Soccer Training Notebook

Soccer Individual Notebook for Continuous Improvement in Free Kicks and Penalty Kicks

Chest Dugger

Free Gift Included

As part of our dedication to help you succeed in your career, we have sent you a free soccer drills worksheet. This is the "Soccer Training Work Sheet" drill sheet. This is a list of drills that you can use to improve your game; as well as a methodology to track your performance on these drills on a day-to-day basis. We want to get you to the next level.

Click on the link below to get your free drills.

https://soccertrainingabiprod.gr8.com/

ABOUT THE AUTHOR

Chest Dugger is a pen name for our soccer coaching brand, Abiprod. We provide high quality soccer coaching tips, drills, fitness and mentality tips to ensure your success.

We have been fans of the beautiful game for decades. Like every soccer fan around the globe, we watch and play the beautiful game as much as we can. Whether we're fans of Manchester United, Real Madrid, Arsenal or LA Galaxy; we share a common love for the beautiful game.

Through our experiences, we've noticed that there's very little information for the common soccer fan who wants to escalate his game to the next level. Or get their kids started on the way. Too much of the information on the web and outside is too basic.

Being passionate about the game, we want to get the message across to as many people as possible. Through our soccer coaching blog, books and products; we aim to bring high quality soccer coaching to the world. Anyone who's passionate about the beautiful game can use our tactics and strategies.
Here's a link to our author page for other books.

https://www.amazon.com/Chest-Dugger/e/B078L131DT/ref=sr_ntt_srch_lnk_1?qid=1514547441&sr=1-1

DISCLAIMER

Copyright © 2020

All Rights Reserved

No part of this eBook can be transmitted or reproduced in any form including print, electronic, photocopying, scanning, mechanical, or recording without prior written permission from the author.

While the author has taken the utmost effort to ensure the accuracy of the written content, all readers are advised to follow information mentioned herein at their own risk. The author cannot be held responsible for any personal or commercial damage caused by information. All readers are encouraged to seek professional advice when needed.

Soccer Free Kick Log

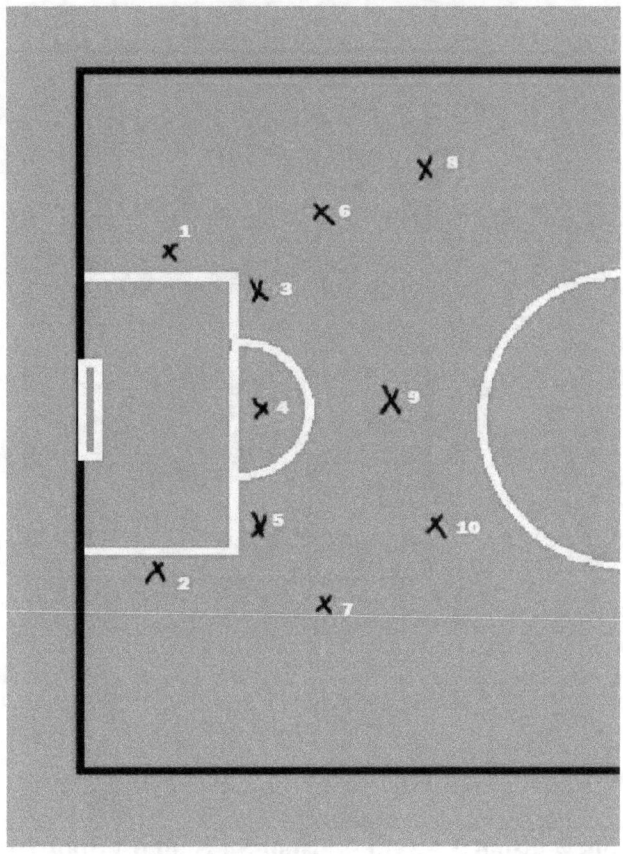

Date:

	Spot 1	Spot 2	Spot 3	Spot 4	Spot 5	Spot 6	Spot 7	Spot 8	Spot 9	Spot 10
Scored										
Missed										
Saved										

Soccer Free Kick Log Example

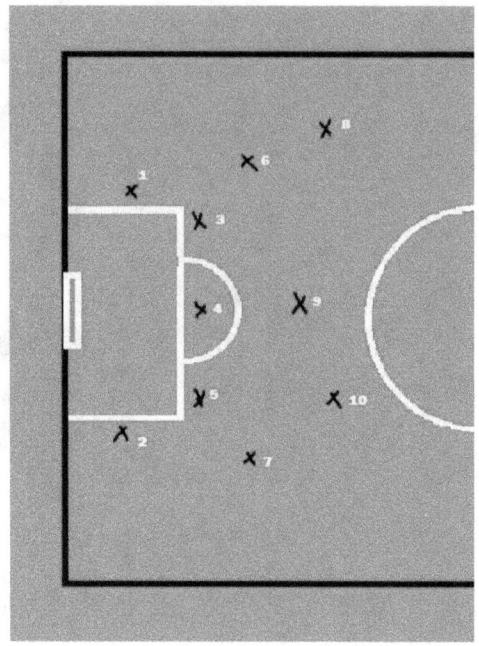

Date: June 20th, 2020

	Spot 1	Spot 2	Spot 3	Spot 4	Spot 5	Spot 6	Spot 7	Spot 8	Spot 9	Spot 10
Scored	3	4	5	6	5	4	3	2	2	1
Missed	2	2	1	2	5	6	4	5	5	4
Saved	7	8	5	8	9	6	7	6	7	6

Scored: You score a goal past the goalkeeper.

Missed: You were off target with your shot.

Saved: Saved by the goalkeeper.

Work on improving your performance over time; reducing the percentage of missed and saved shots.

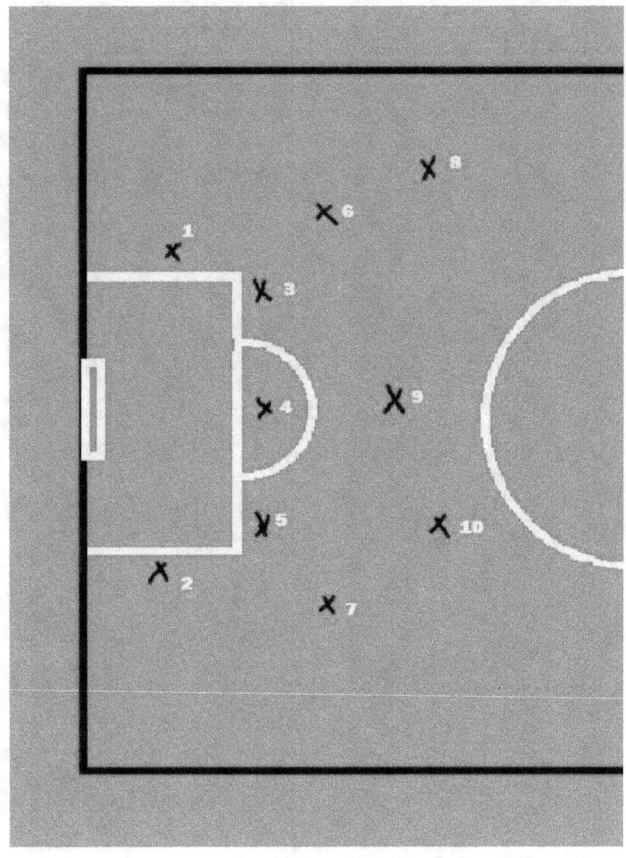

Date:

	Spot 1	Spot 2	Spot 3	Spot 4	Spot 5	Spot 6	Spot 7	Spot 8	Spot 9	Spot 10
Scored										
Missed										
Saved										

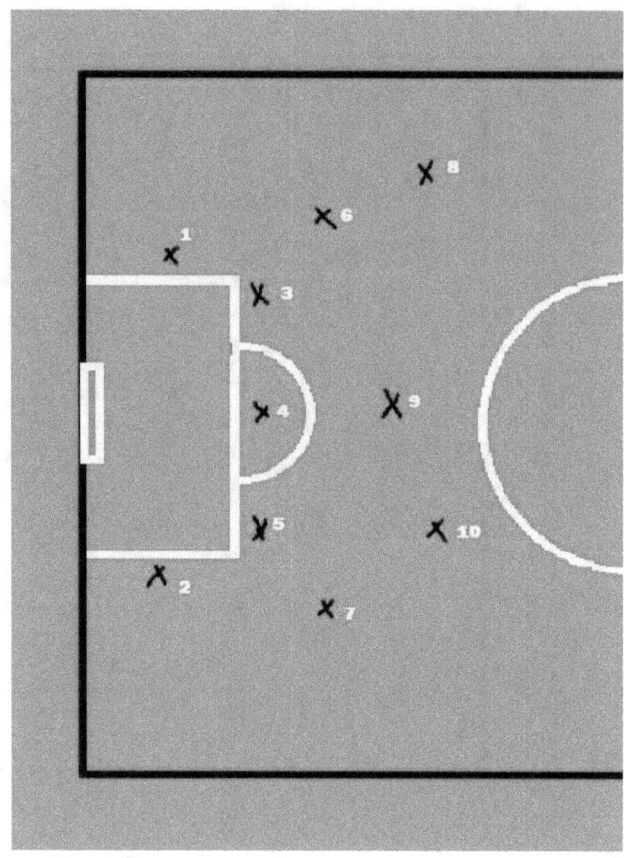

Date:

	Spot 1	Spot 2	Spot 3	Spot 4	Spot 5	Spot 6	Spot 7	Spot 8	Spot 9	Spot 10
Scored										
Missed										
Saved										

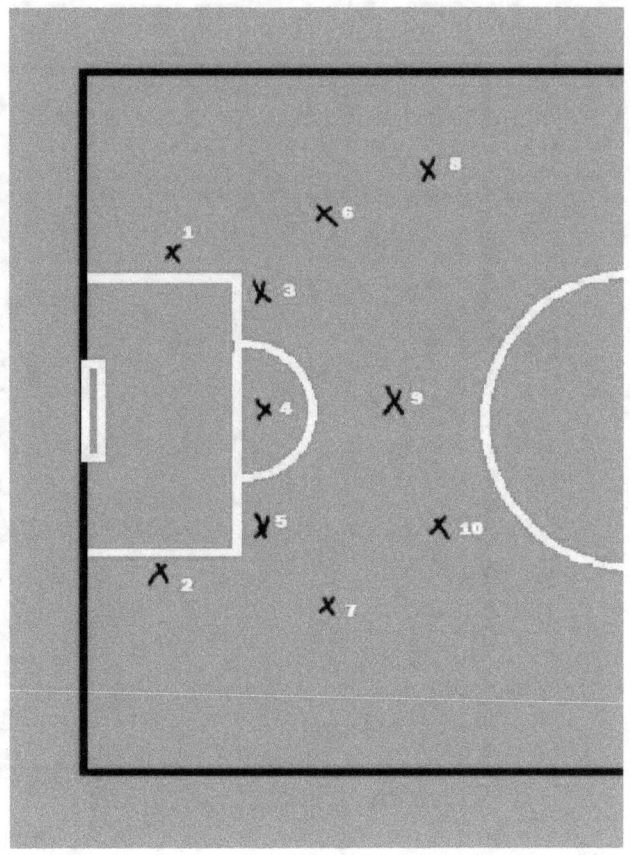

Date:

	Spot 1	Spot 2	Spot 3	Spot 4	Spot 5	Spot 6	Spot 7	Spot 8	Spot 9	Spot 10
Scored										
Missed										
Saved										

Date:

	Spot 1	Spot 2	Spot 3	Spot 4	Spot 5	Spot 6	Spot 7	Spot 8	Spot 9	Spot 10
Scored										
Missed										
Saved										

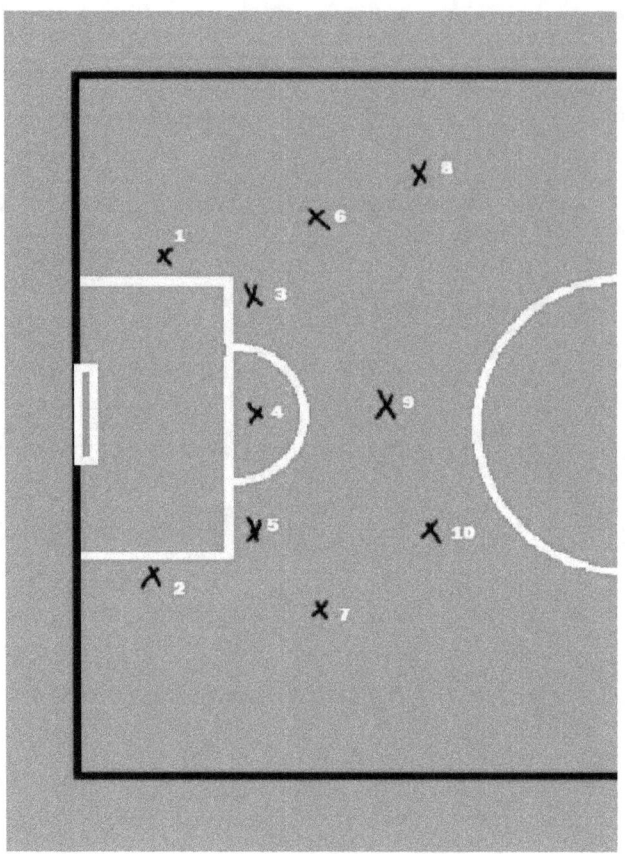

Date:

	Spot 1	Spot 2	Spot 3	Spot 4	Spot 5	Spot 6	Spot 7	Spot 8	Spot 9	Spot 10
Scored										
Missed										
Saved										

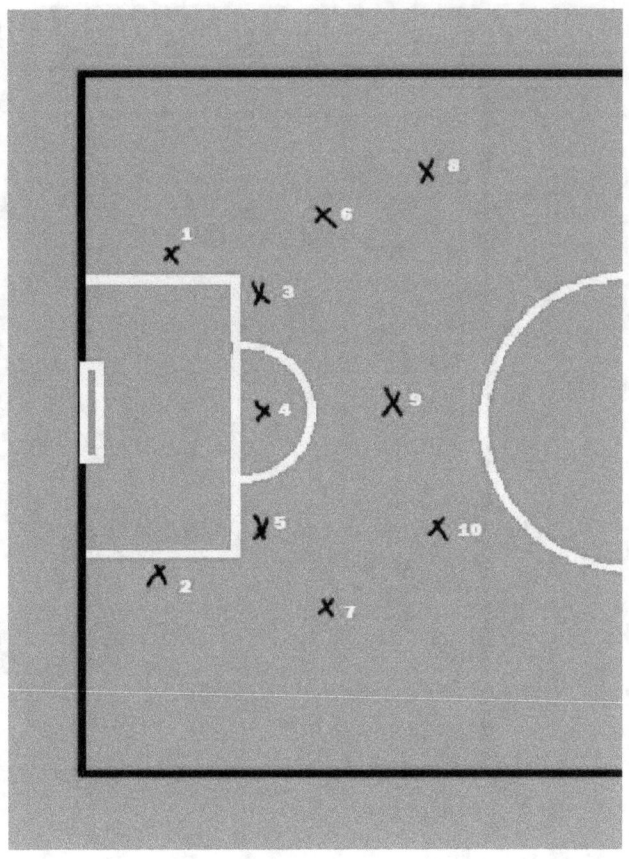

Date:

	Spot 1	Spot 2	Spot 3	Spot 4	Spot 5	Spot 6	Spot 7	Spot 8	Spot 9	Spot 10
Scored										
Missed										
Saved										

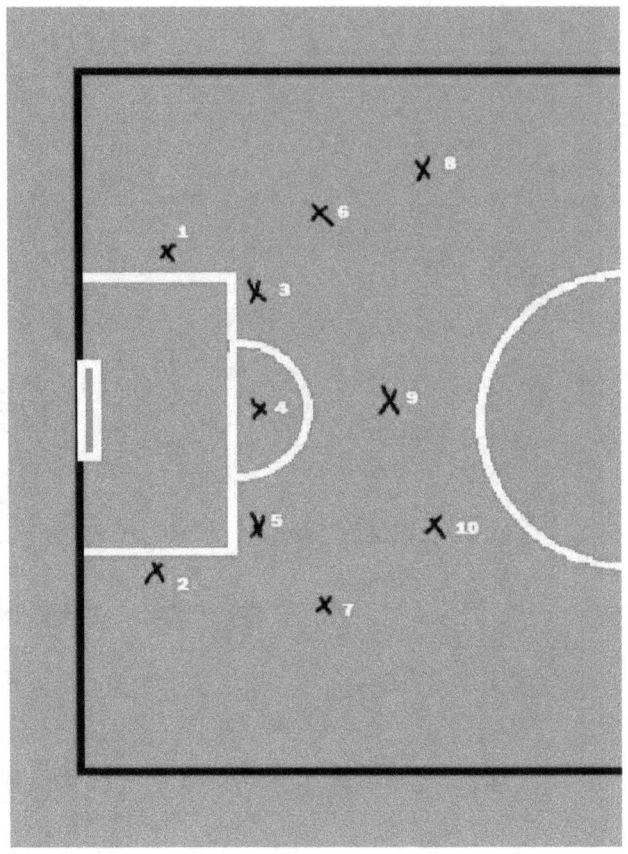

Date:

	Spot 1	Spot 2	Spot 3	Spot 4	Spot 5	Spot 6	Spot 7	Spot 8	Spot 9	Spot 10
Scored										
Missed										
Saved										

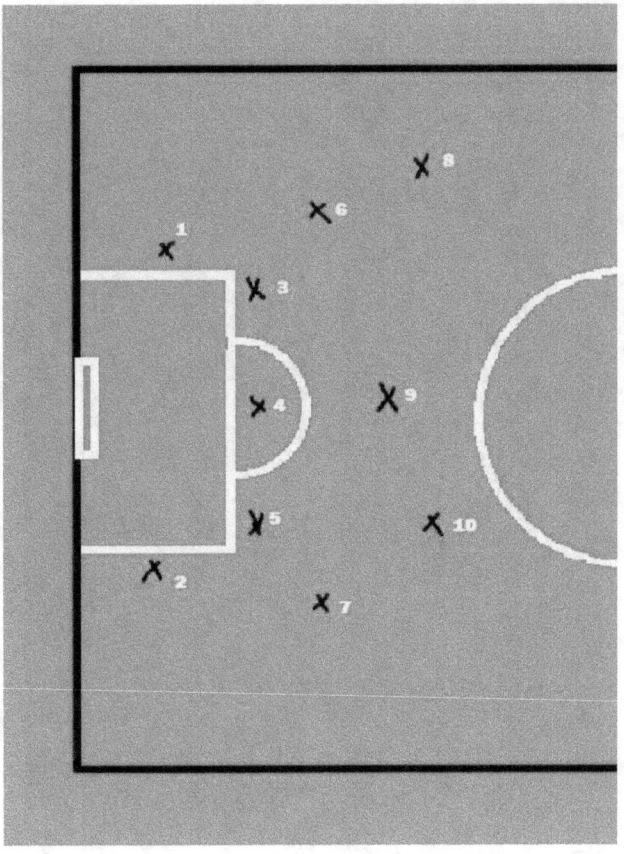

Date:

	Spot 1	Spot 2	Spot 3	Spot 4	Spot 5	Spot 6	Spot 7	Spot 8	Spot 9	Spot 10
Scored										
Missed										
Saved										

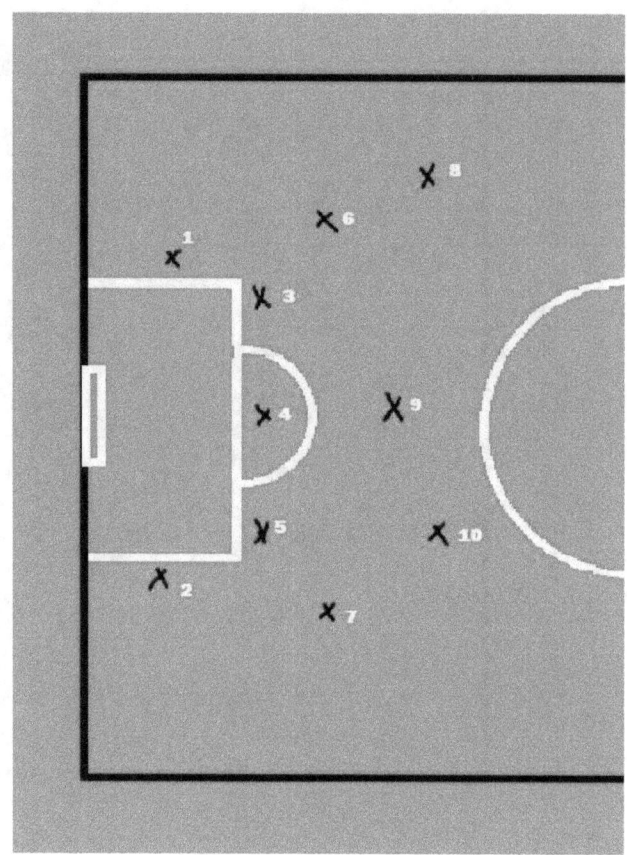

Date:

	Spot 1	Spot 2	Spot 3	Spot 4	Spot 5	Spot 6	Spot 7	Spot 8	Spot 9	Spot 10
Scored										
Missed										
Saved										

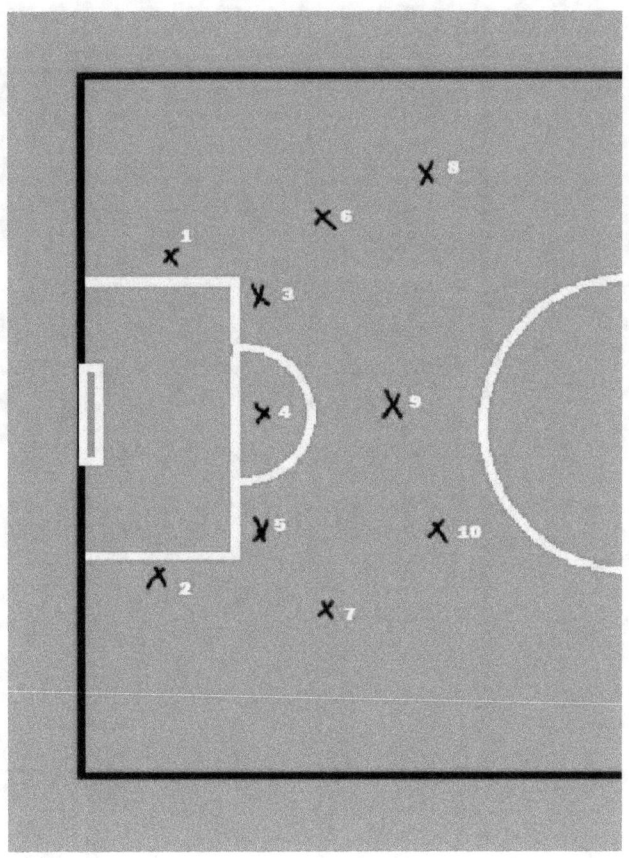

Date:

	Spot 1	Spot 2	Spot 3	Spot 4	Spot 5	Spot 6	Spot 7	Spot 8	Spot 9	Spot 10
Scored										
Missed										
Saved										

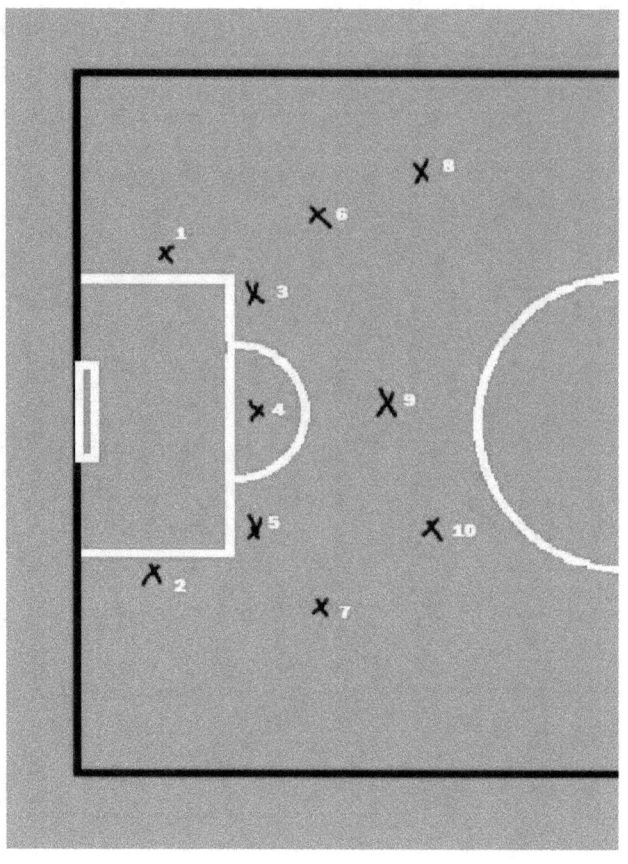

Date:

	Spot 1	Spot 2	Spot 3	Spot 4	Spot 5	Spot 6	Spot 7	Spot 8	Spot 9	Spot 10
Scored										
Missed										
Saved										

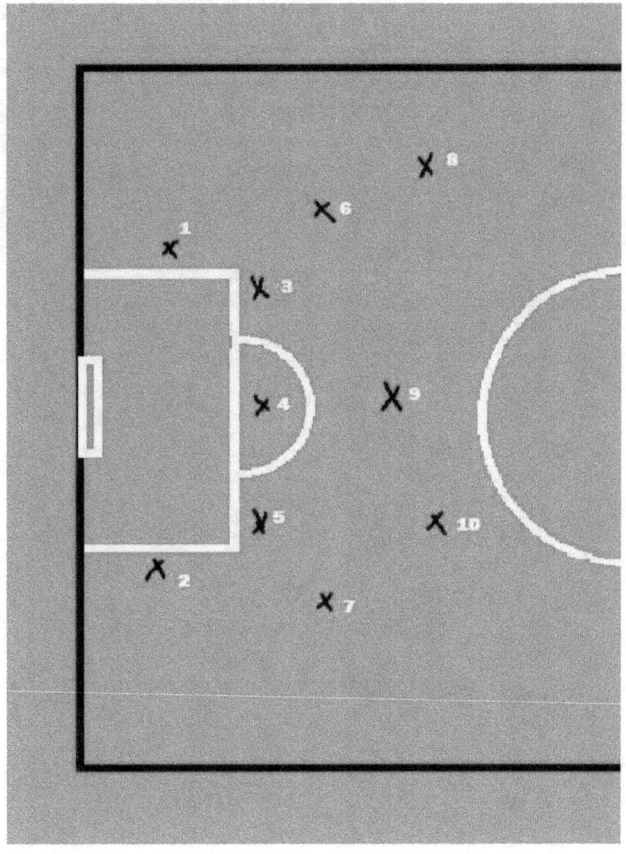

Date:

	Spot 1	Spot 2	Spot 3	Spot 4	Spot 5	Spot 6	Spot 7	Spot 8	Spot 9	Spot 10
Scored										
Missed										
Saved										

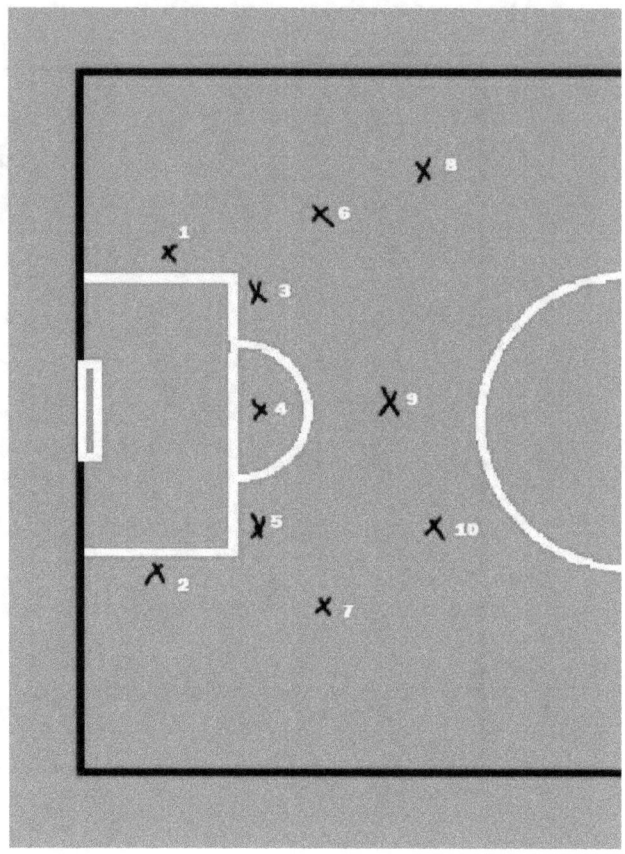

Date:

	Spot 1	Spot 2	Spot 3	Spot 4	Spot 5	Spot 6	Spot 7	Spot 8	Spot 9	Spot 10
Scored										
Missed										
Saved										

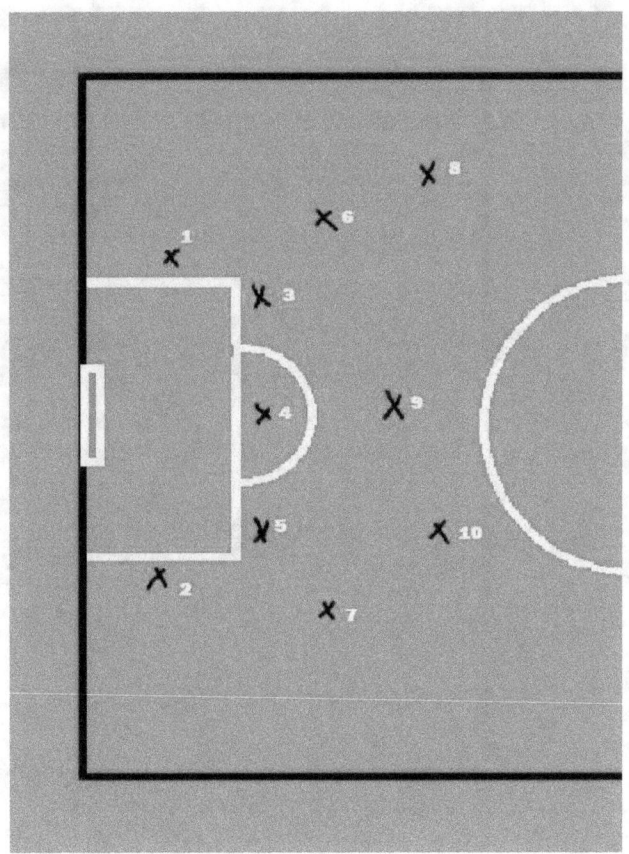

Date:

	Spot 1	Spot 2	Spot 3	Spot 4	Spot 5	Spot 6	Spot 7	Spot 8	Spot 9	Spot 10
Scored										
Missed										
Saved										

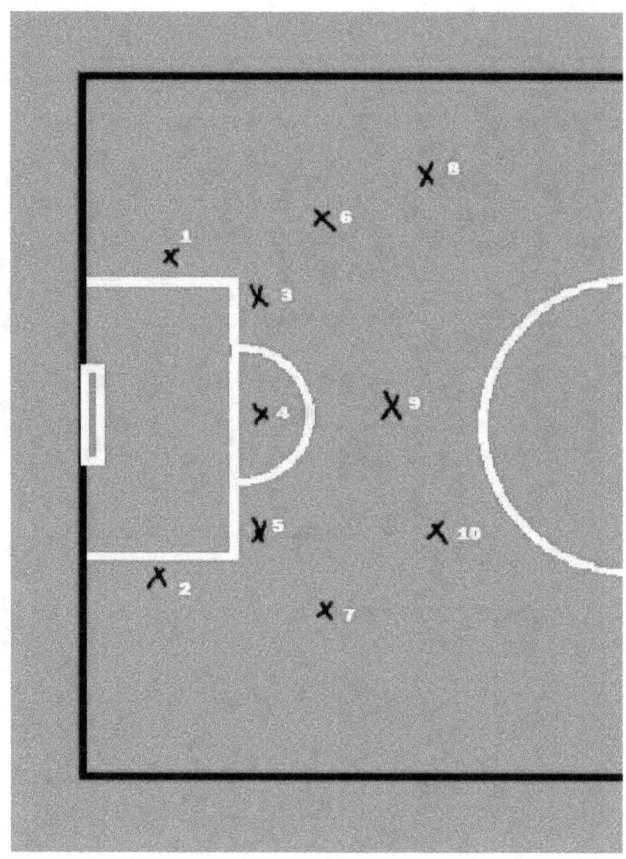

Date:

	Spot 1	Spot 2	Spot 3	Spot 4	Spot 5	Spot 6	Spot 7	Spot 8	Spot 9	Spot 10
Scored										
Missed										
Saved										

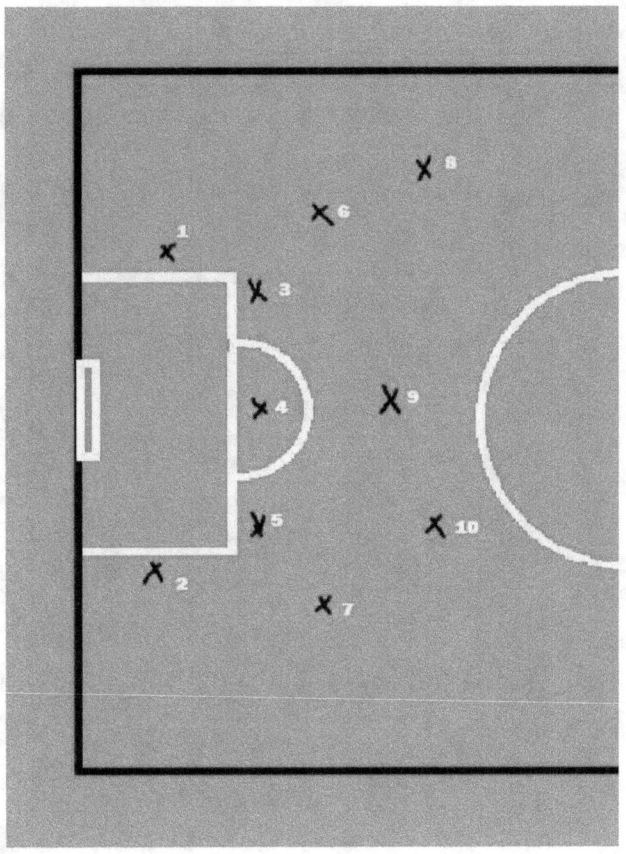

Date:

	Spot 1	Spot 2	Spot 3	Spot 4	Spot 5	Spot 6	Spot 7	Spot 8	Spot 9	Spot 10
Scored										
Missed										
Saved										

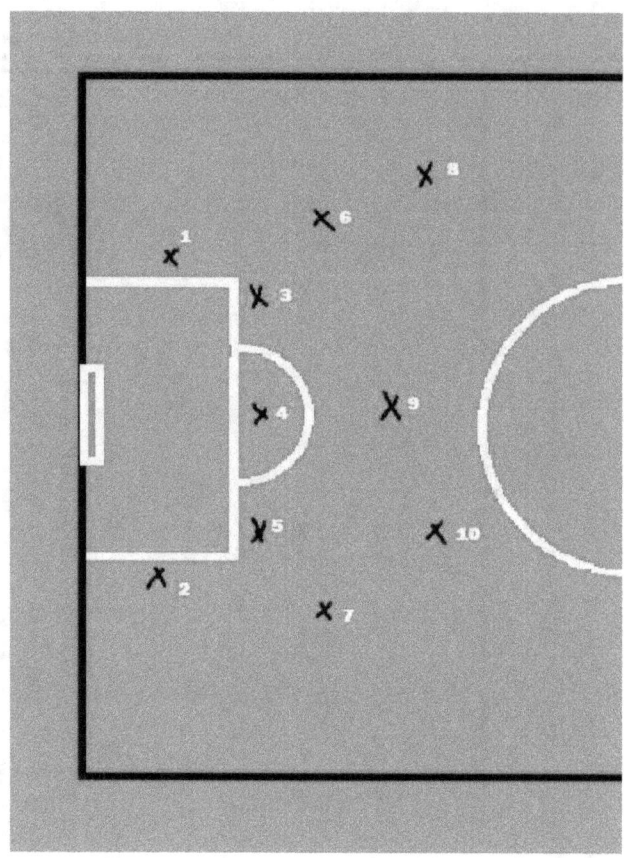

Date:

	Spot 1	Spot 2	Spot 3	Spot 4	Spot 5	Spot 6	Spot 7	Spot 8	Spot 9	Spot 10
Scored										
Missed										
Saved										

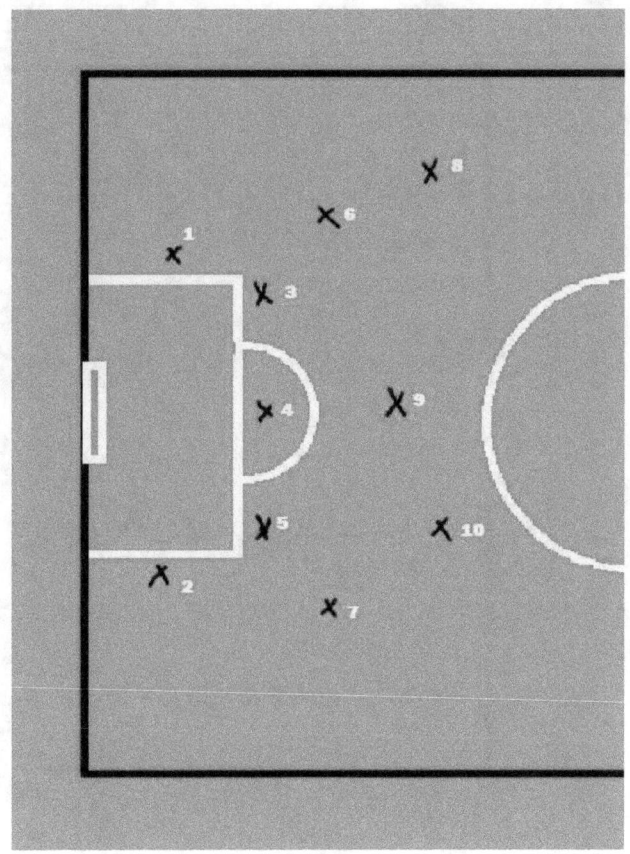

Date:

	Spot 1	Spot 2	Spot 3	Spot 4	Spot 5	Spot 6	Spot 7	Spot 8	Spot 9	Spot 10
Scored										
Missed										
Saved										

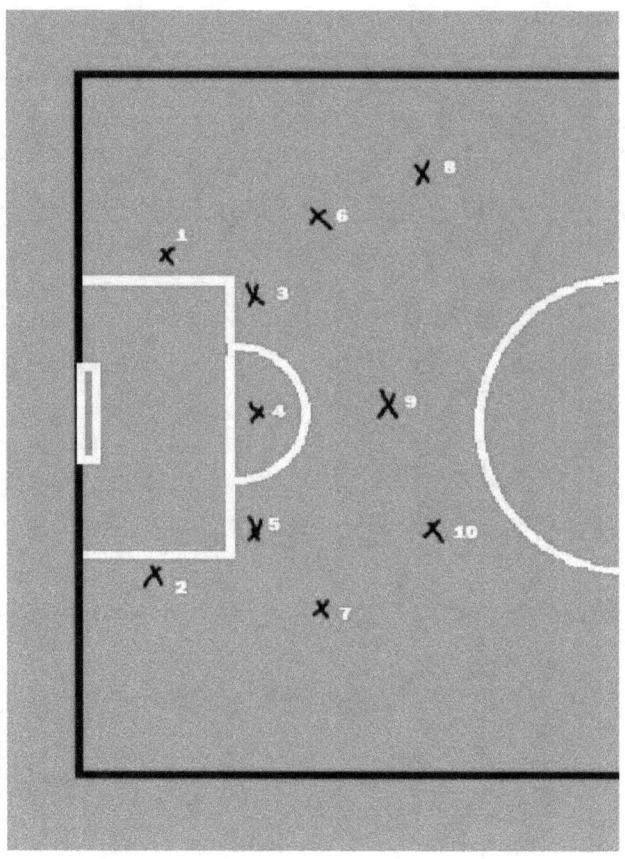

Date:

	Spot 1	Spot 2	Spot 3	Spot 4	Spot 5	Spot 6	Spot 7	Spot 8	Spot 9	Spot 10
Scored										
Missed										
Saved										

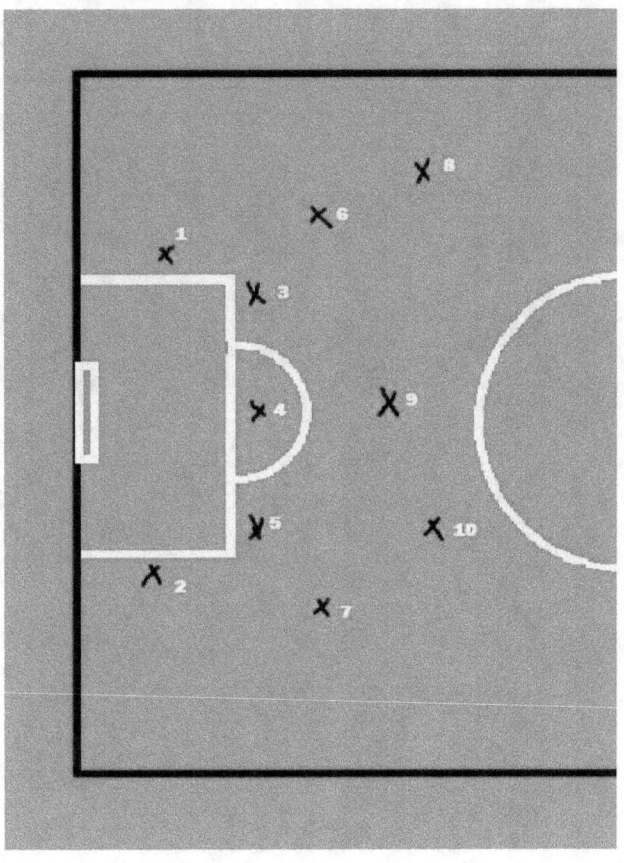

Date:

	Spot 1	Spot 2	Spot 3	Spot 4	Spot 5	Spot 6	Spot 7	Spot 8	Spot 9	Spot 10
Scored										
Missed										
Saved										

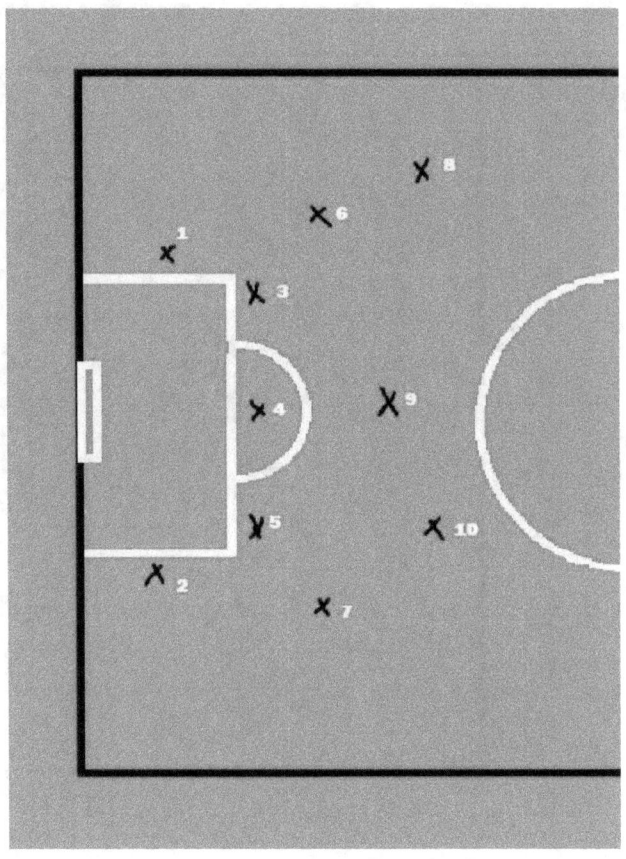

Date:

	Spot 1	Spot 2	Spot 3	Spot 4	Spot 5	Spot 6	Spot 7	Spot 8	Spot 9	Spot 10
Scored										
Missed										
Saved										

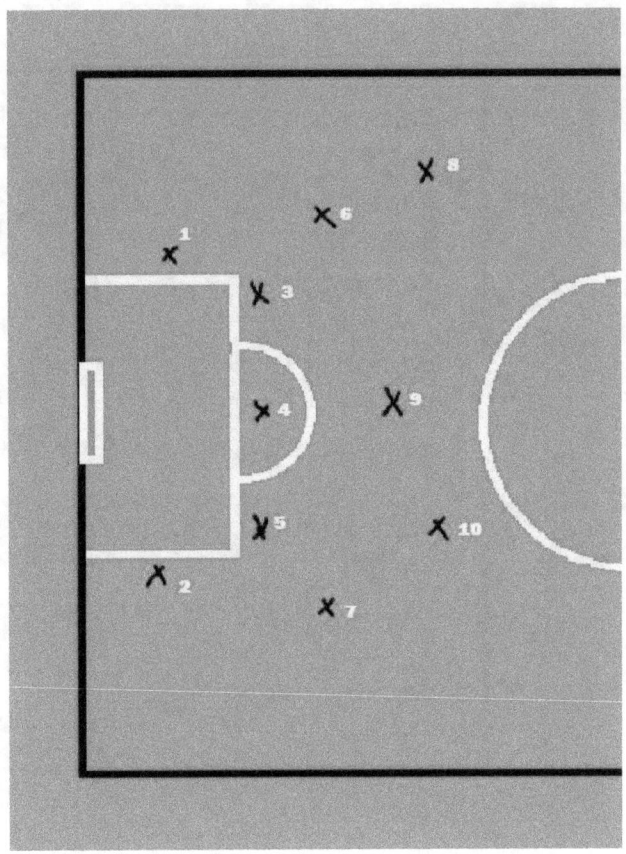

Date:

	Spot 1	Spot 2	Spot 3	Spot 4	Spot 5	Spot 6	Spot 7	Spot 8	Spot 9	Spot 10
Scored										
Missed										
Saved										

Date:

	Spot 1	Spot 2	Spot 3	Spot 4	Spot 5	Spot 6	Spot 7	Spot 8	Spot 9	Spot 10
Scored										
Missed										
Saved										

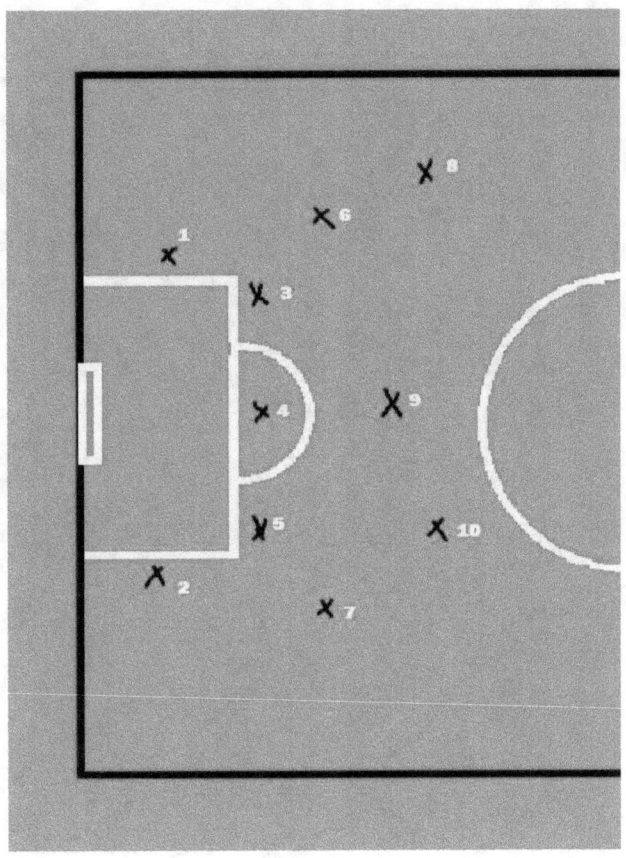

Date:

	Spot 1	Spot 2	Spot 3	Spot 4	Spot 5	Spot 6	Spot 7	Spot 8	Spot 9	Spot 10
Scored										
Missed										
Saved										

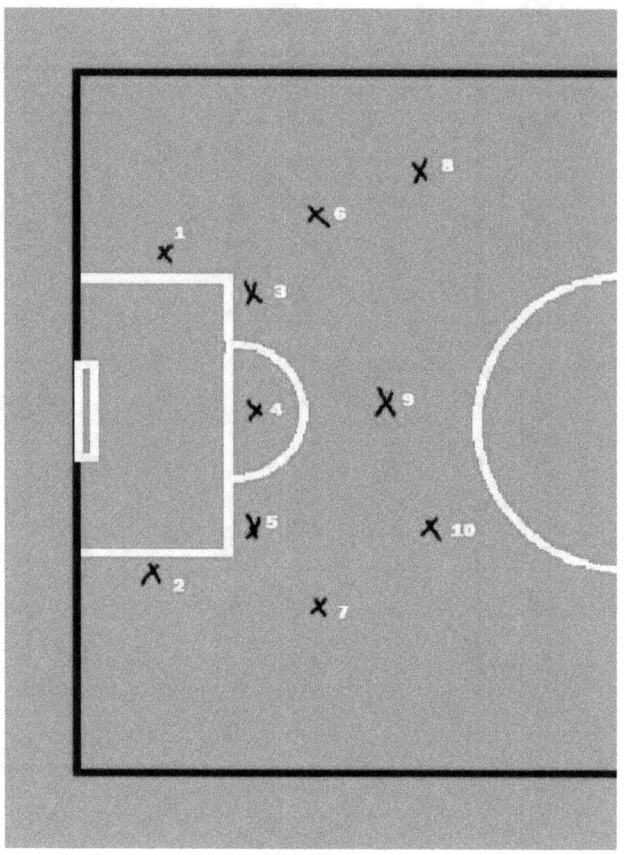

Date:

	Spot 1	Spot 2	Spot 3	Spot 4	Spot 5	Spot 6	Spot 7	Spot 8	Spot 9	Spot 10
Scored										
Missed										
Saved										

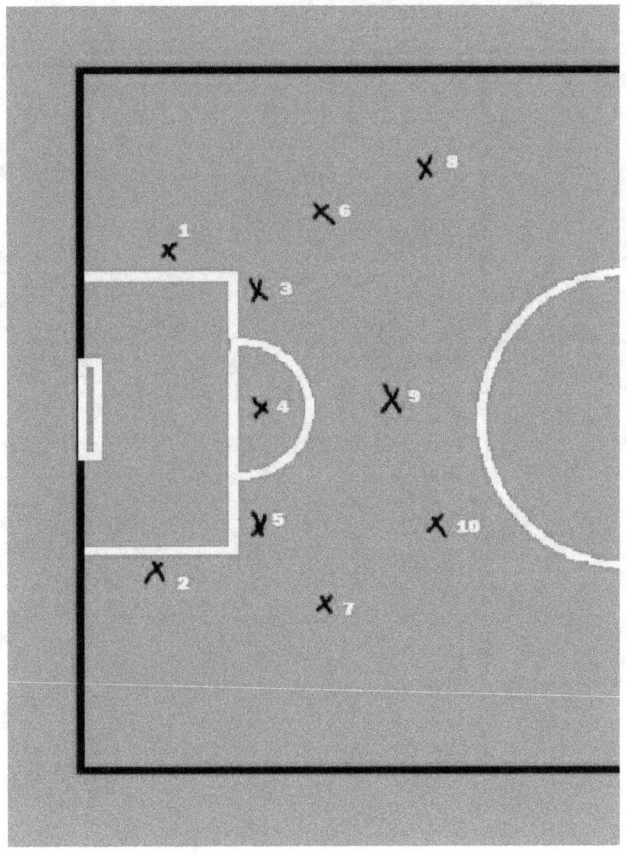

Date:

	Spot 1	Spot 2	Spot 3	Spot 4	Spot 5	Spot 6	Spot 7	Spot 8	Spot 9	Spot 10
Scored										
Missed										
Saved										

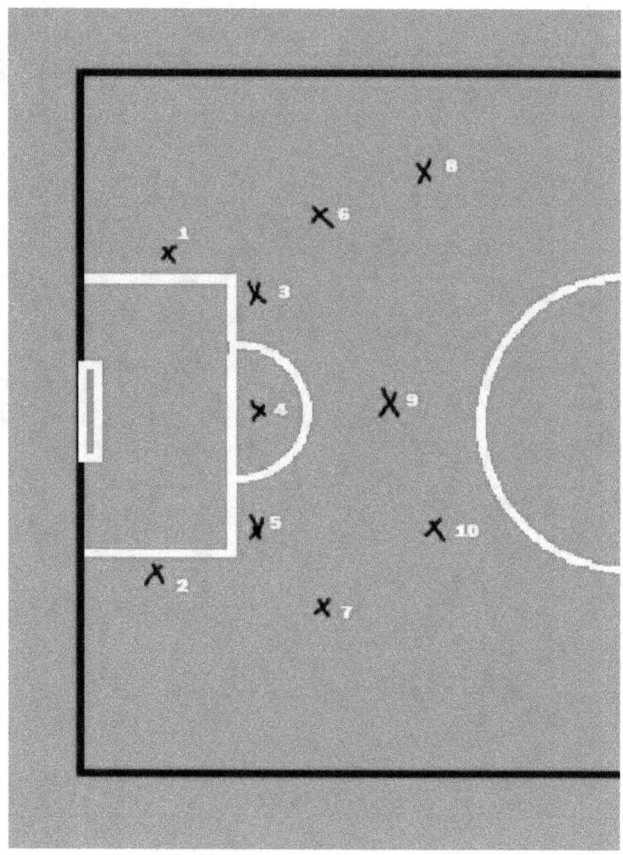

Date:

	Spot 1	Spot 2	Spot 3	Spot 4	Spot 5	Spot 6	Spot 7	Spot 8	Spot 9	Spot 10
Scored										
Missed										
Saved										

Date:

	Spot 1	Spot 2	Spot 3	Spot 4	Spot 5	Spot 6	Spot 7	Spot 8	Spot 9	Spot 10
Scored										
Missed										
Saved										

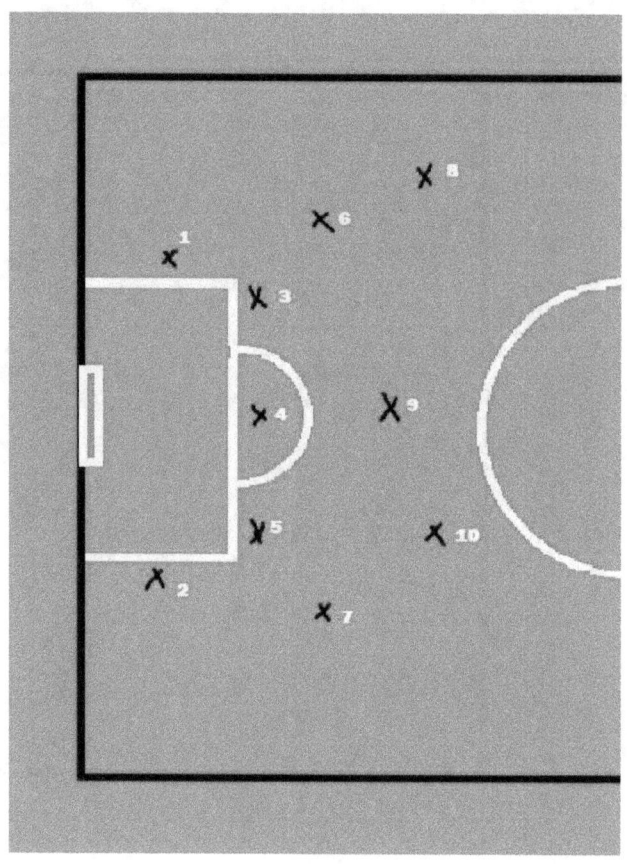

Date:

	Spot 1	Spot 2	Spot 3	Spot 4	Spot 5	Spot 6	Spot 7	Spot 8	Spot 9	Spot 10
Scored										
Missed										
Saved										

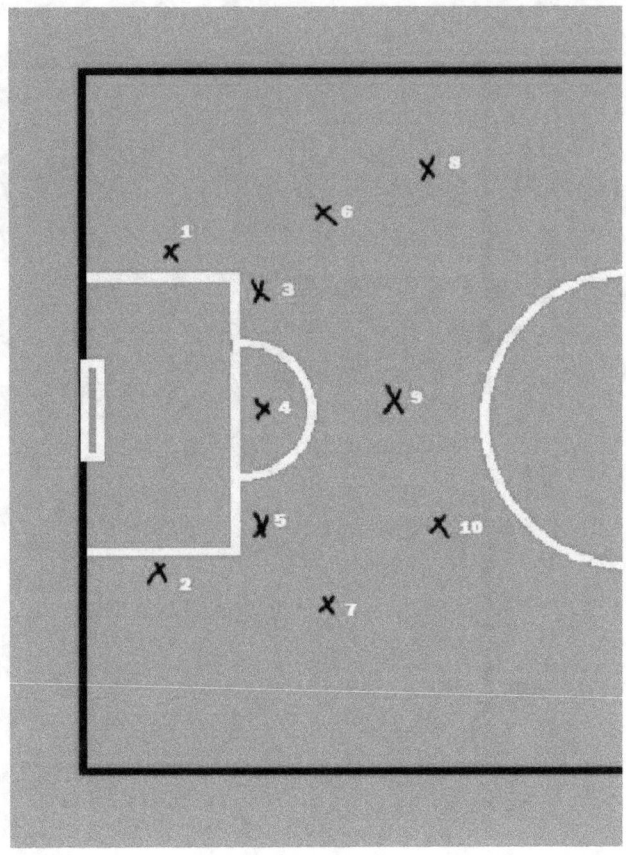

Date:

	Spot 1	Spot 2	Spot 3	Spot 4	Spot 5	Spot 6	Spot 7	Spot 8	Spot 9	Spot 10
Scored										
Missed										
Saved										

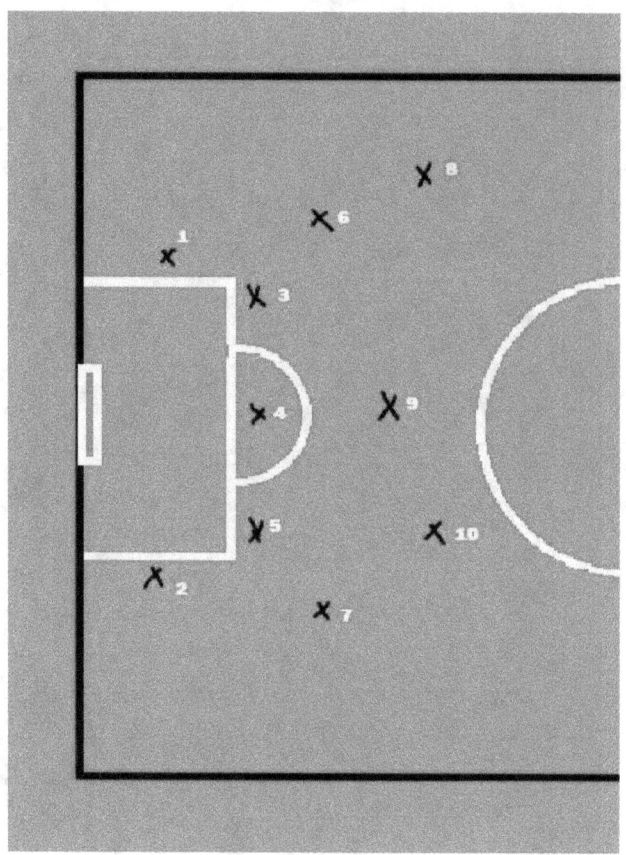

Date:

	Spot 1	Spot 2	Spot 3	Spot 4	Spot 5	Spot 6	Spot 7	Spot 8	Spot 9	Spot 10
Scored										
Missed										
Saved										

Date:

	Spot 1	Spot 2	Spot 3	Spot 4	Spot 5	Spot 6	Spot 7	Spot 8	Spot 9	Spot 10
Scored										
Missed										
Saved										

Date:

	Spot 1	Spot 2	Spot 3	Spot 4	Spot 5	Spot 6	Spot 7	Spot 8	Spot 9	Spot 10
Scored										
Missed										
Saved										

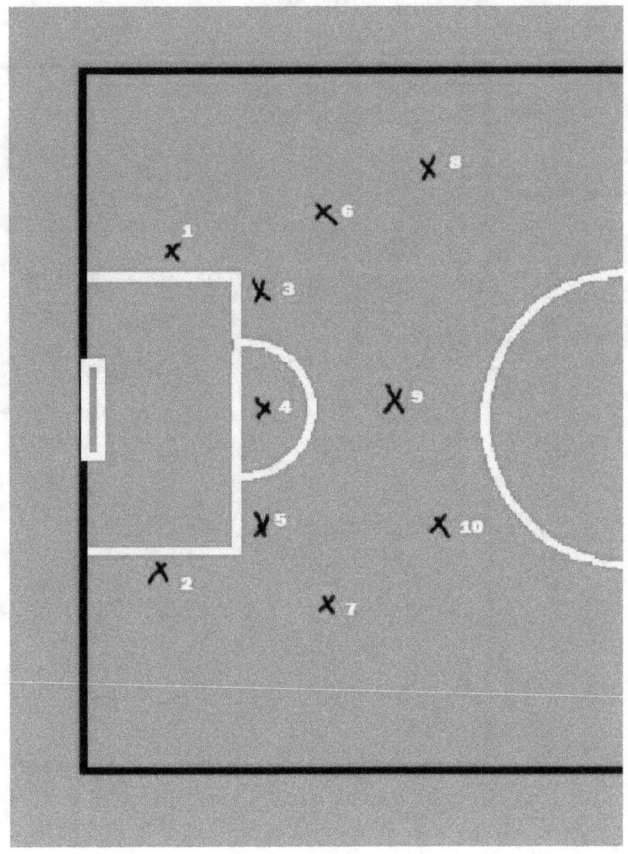

Date:

	Spot 1	Spot 2	Spot 3	Spot 4	Spot 5	Spot 6	Spot 7	Spot 8	Spot 9	Spot 10
Scored										
Missed										
Saved										

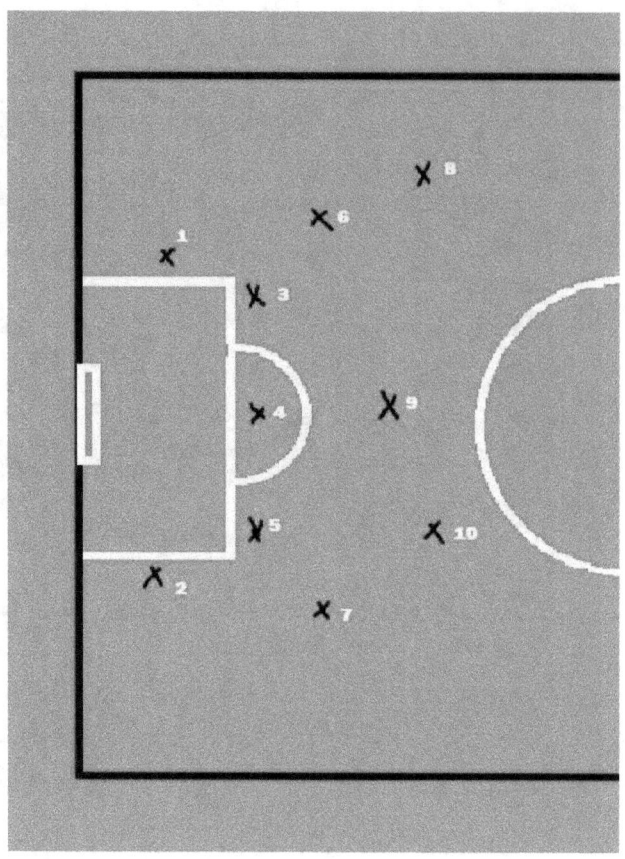

Date:

	Spot 1	Spot 2	Spot 3	Spot 4	Spot 5	Spot 6	Spot 7	Spot 8	Spot 9	Spot 10
Scored										
Missed										
Saved										

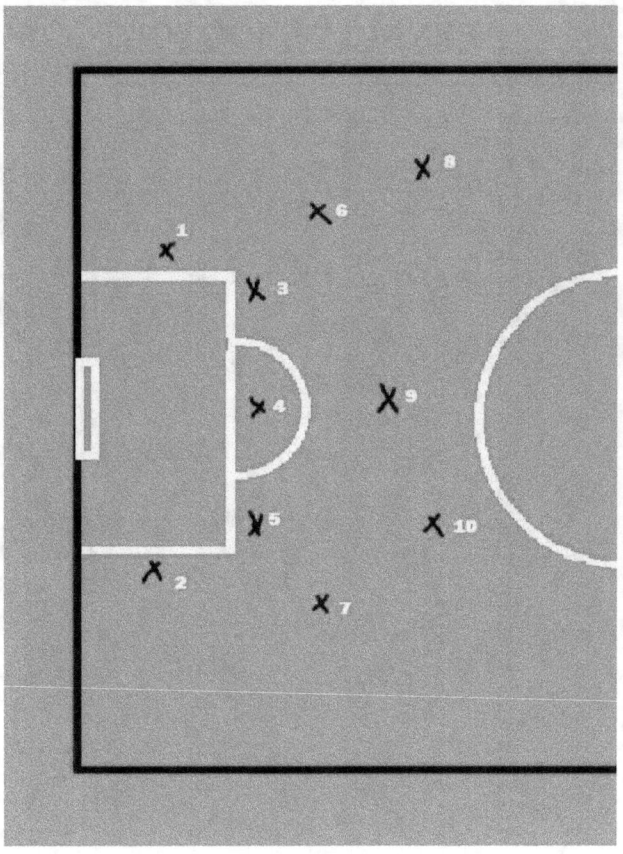

Date:

	Spot 1	Spot 2	Spot 3	Spot 4	Spot 5	Spot 6	Spot 7	Spot 8	Spot 9	Spot 10
Scored										
Missed										
Saved										

PENALTY SHOOTOUT LOG

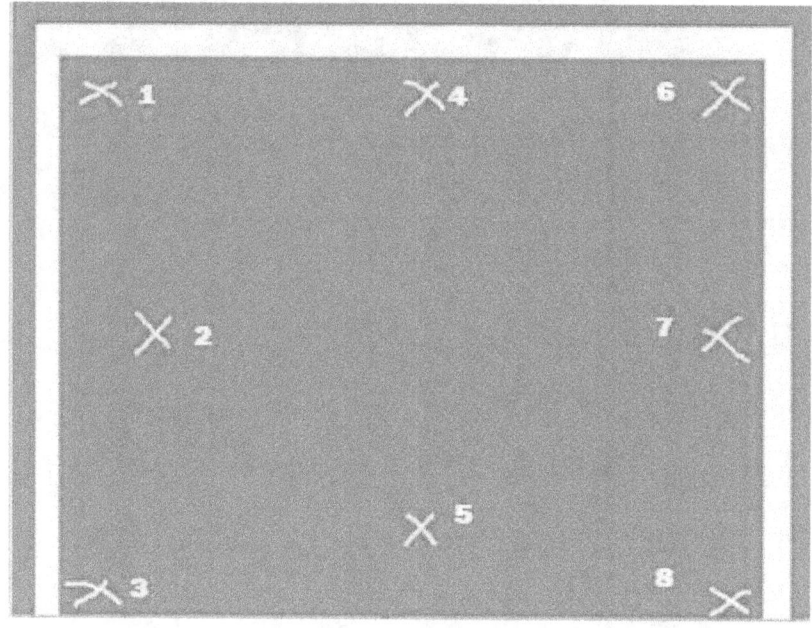

Date:

	Spot 1	Spot 2	Spot 3	Spot 4	Spot 5	Spot 6	Spot 7	Spot 8
Hit area and scored								
Hit area and saved								
Missed area								

PENALTY SHOOTOUT LOG - EXAMPLE

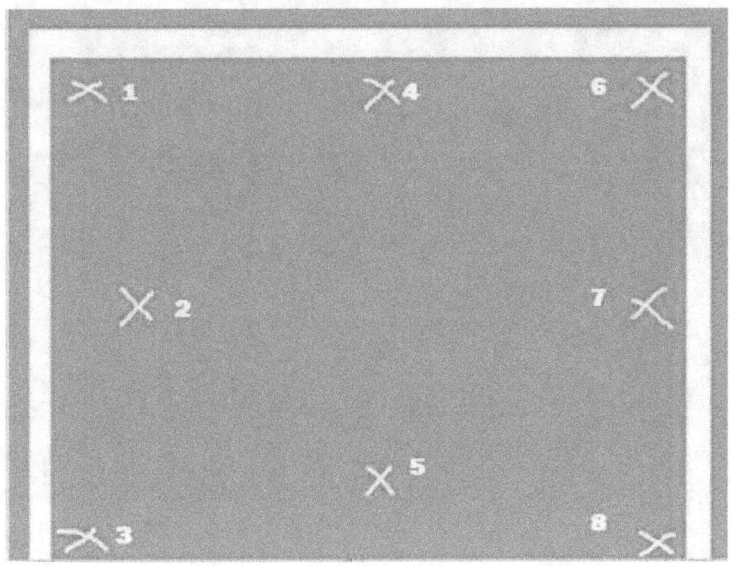

Date:

	Spot 1	Spot 2	Spot 3	Spot 4	Spot 5	Spot 6	Spot 7	Spot 8
Hit Area and Scored	7	8	6	3	6	5	6	6
Hit Area and Saved	4	3	4	7	7	6	2	3
Missed Area	4	5	6	3	3	7	7	7

Hit Area and Scored = You hit the exact area of the goal you were aiming for, and also got it past the goalkeeper.

Hit Area and Saved = You hit the exact area of the goal you were aiming for, but the goalkeeper saved it. Work on increasing power or hiding intent from goalkeeper.

Missed Area = You couldn't get the ball in the right area. Work on getting the ball in the right spot.

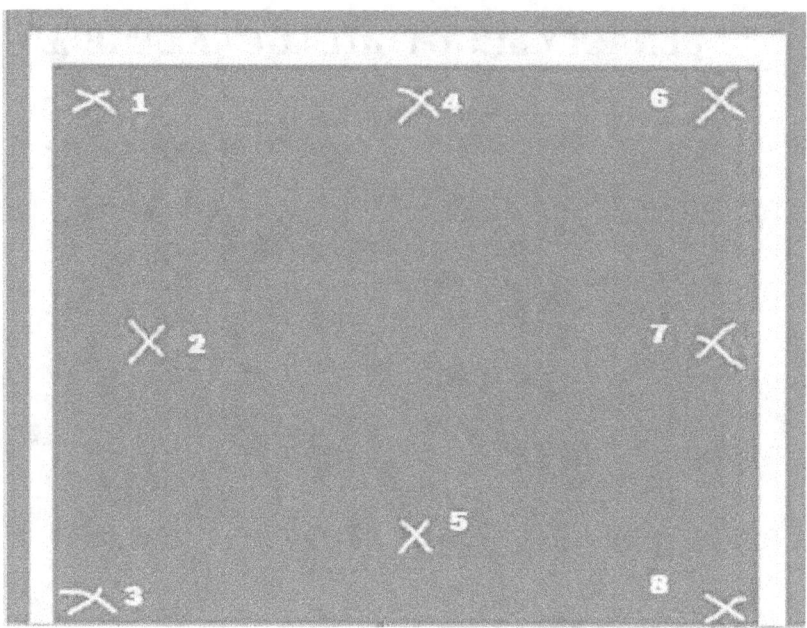

Date:

	Spot 1	Spot 2	Spot 3	Spot 4	Spot 5	Spot 6	Spot 7	Spot 8
Hit area and scored								
Hit area and saved								
Missed area								

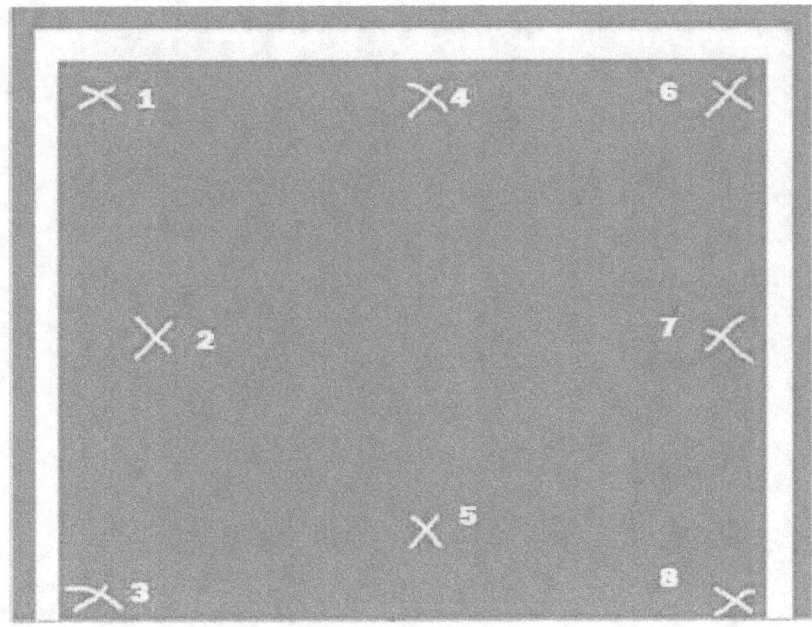

Date:

	Spot 1	Spot 2	Spot 3	Spot 4	Spot 5	Spot 6	Spot 7	Spot 8
Hit area and scored								
Hit area and saved								
Missed area								

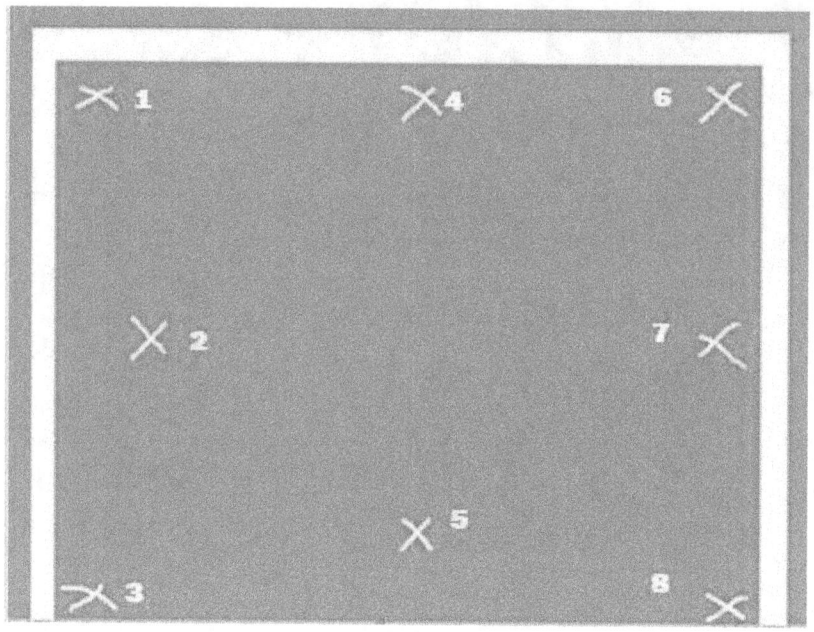

Date:

	Spot 1	Spot 2	Spot 3	Spot 4	Spot 5	Spot 6	Spot 7	Spot 8
Hit area and scored								
Hit area and saved								
Missed area								

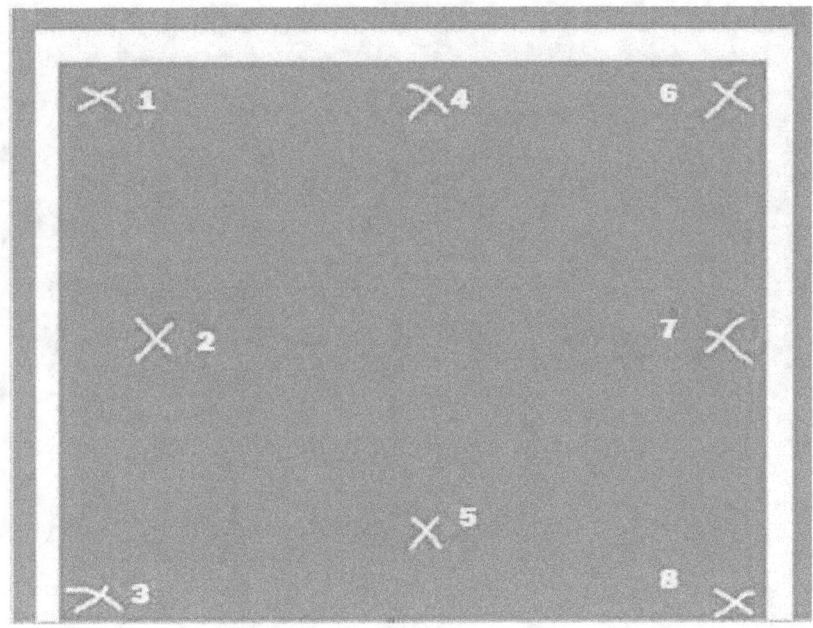

Date:

	Spot 1	Spot 2	Spot 3	Spot 4	Spot 5	Spot 6	Spot 7	Spot 8
Hit area and scored								
Hit area and saved								
Missed area								

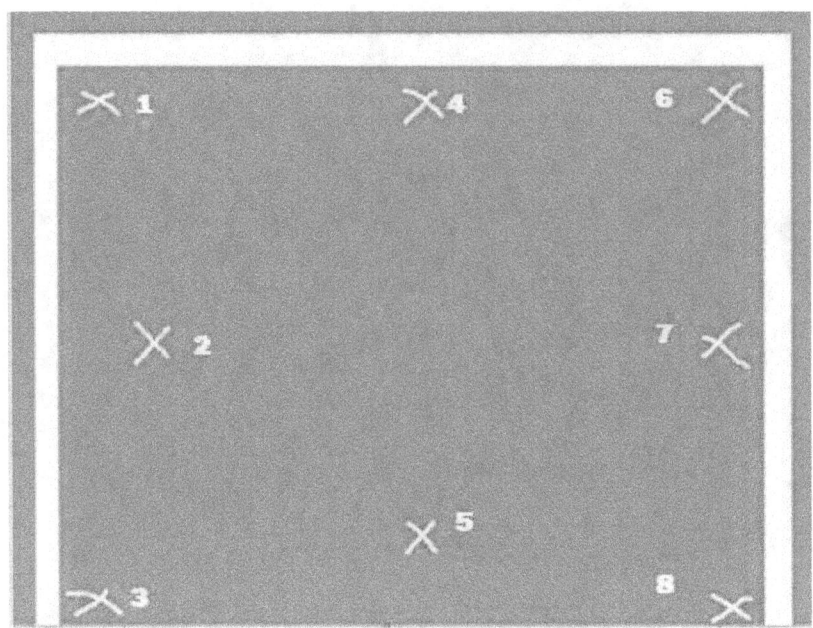

Date:

	Spot 1	Spot 2	Spot 3	Spot 4	Spot 5	Spot 6	Spot 7	Spot 8
Hit area and scored								
Hit area and saved								
Missed area								

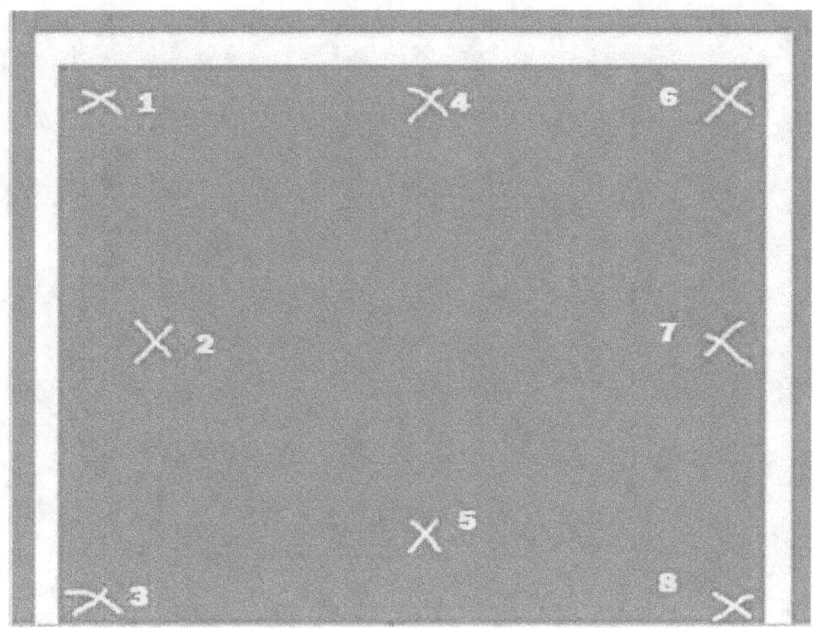

Date:

	Spot 1	Spot 2	Spot 3	Spot 4	Spot 5	Spot 6	Spot 7	Spot 8
Hit area and scored								
Hit area and saved								
Missed area								

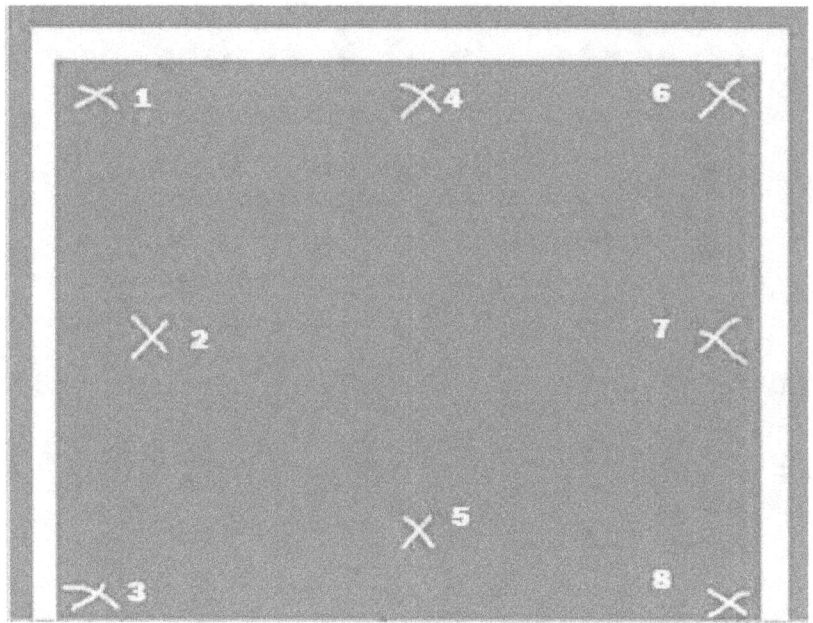

Date:

	Spot 1	Spot 2	Spot 3	Spot 4	Spot 5	Spot 6	Spot 7	Spot 8
Hit area and scored								
Hit area and saved								
Missed area								

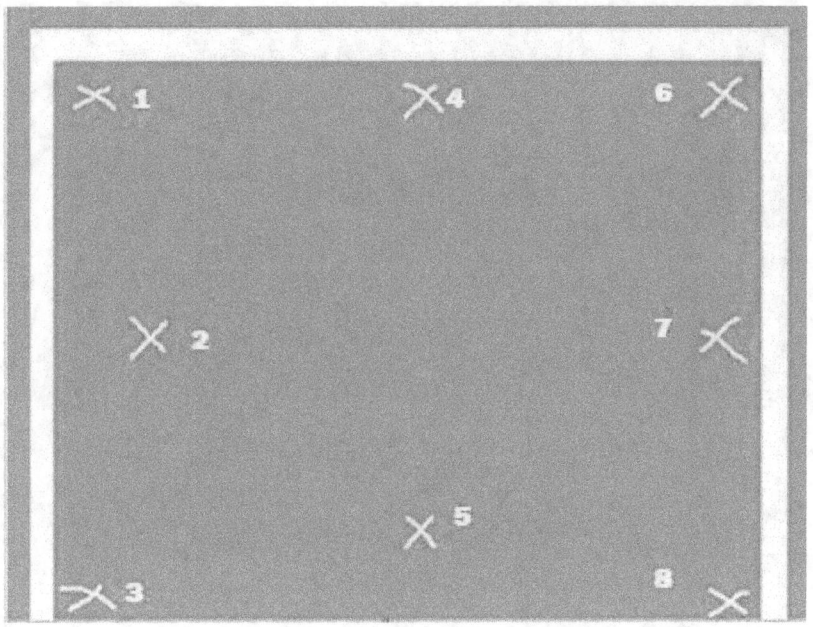

Date:

	Spot 1	Spot 2	Spot 3	Spot 4	Spot 5	Spot 6	Spot 7	Spot 8	Spot 1	Spot 2	Spot 3	Spot 4	Spot 5	Spot 6	Spot 7	Spot 8
Hit area and scored																
Hit area and saved																
Missed area																

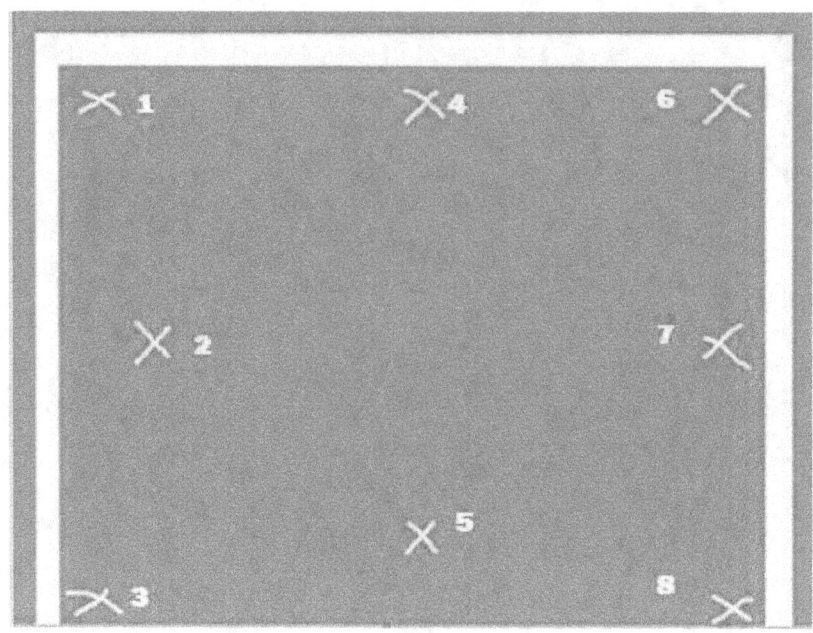

Date:

	Spot 1	Spot 2	Spot 3	Spot 4	Spot 5	Spot 6	Spot 7	Spot 8
Hit area and scored								
Hit area and saved								
Missed area								

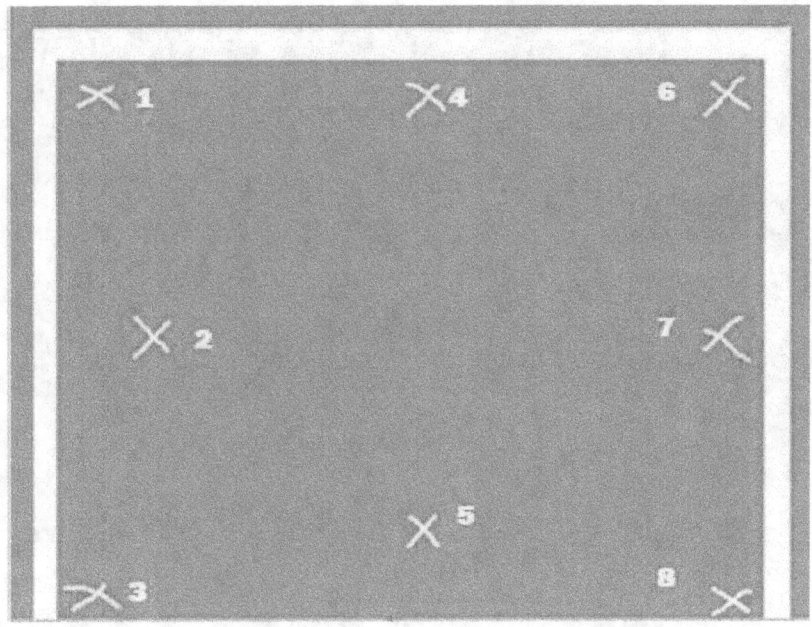

Date:

	Spot 1	Spot 2	Spot 3	Spot 4	Spot 5	Spot 6	Spot 7	Spot 8
Hit area and scored								
Hit area and saved								
Missed area								

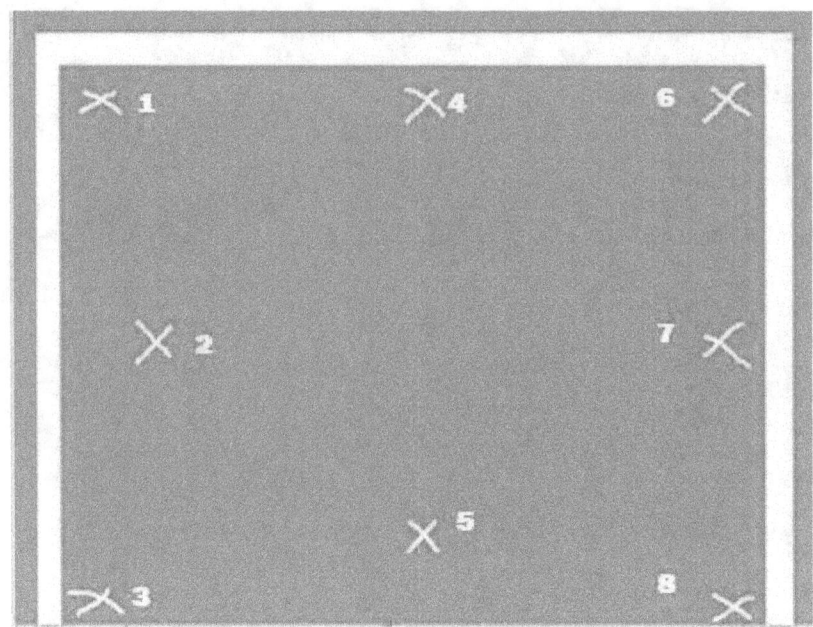

Date:

	Spot 1	Spot 2	Spot 3	Spot 4	Spot 5	Spot 6	Spot 7	Spot 8
Hit area and scored								
Hit area and saved								
Missed area								

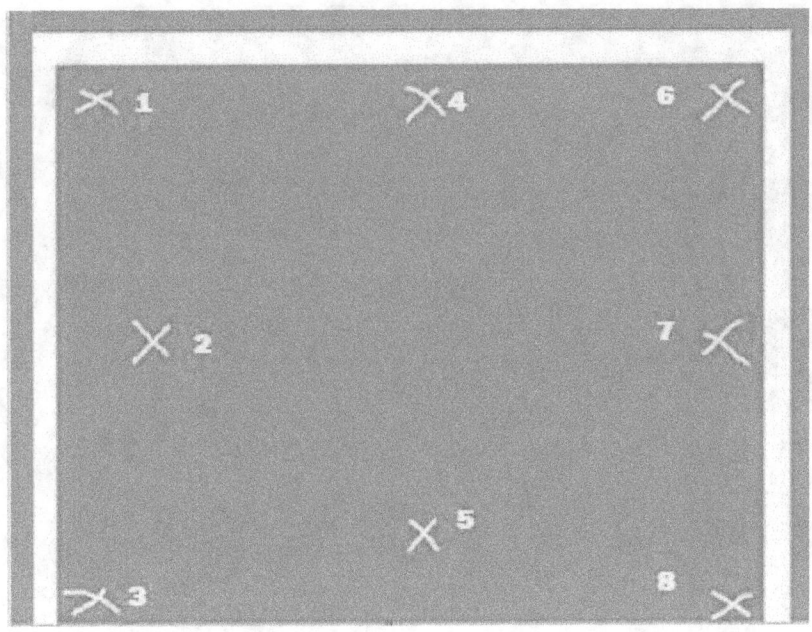

Date:

	Spot 1	Spot 2	Spot 3	Spot 4	Spot 5	Spot 6	Spot 7	Spot 8
Hit area and scored								
Hit area and saved								
Missed area								

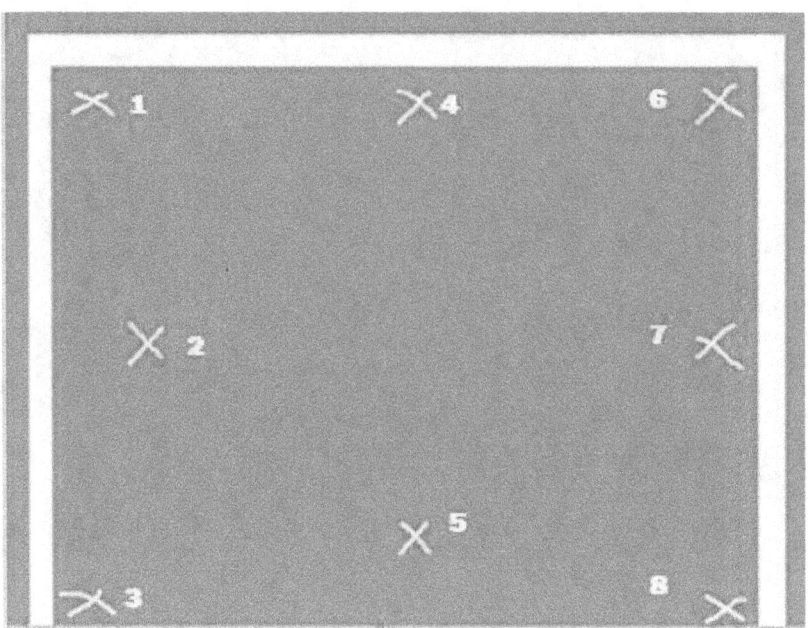

Date:

	Spot 1	Spot 2	Spot 3	Spot 4	Spot 5	Spot 6	Spot 7	Spot 8
Hit area and scored								
Hit area and saved								
Missed area								

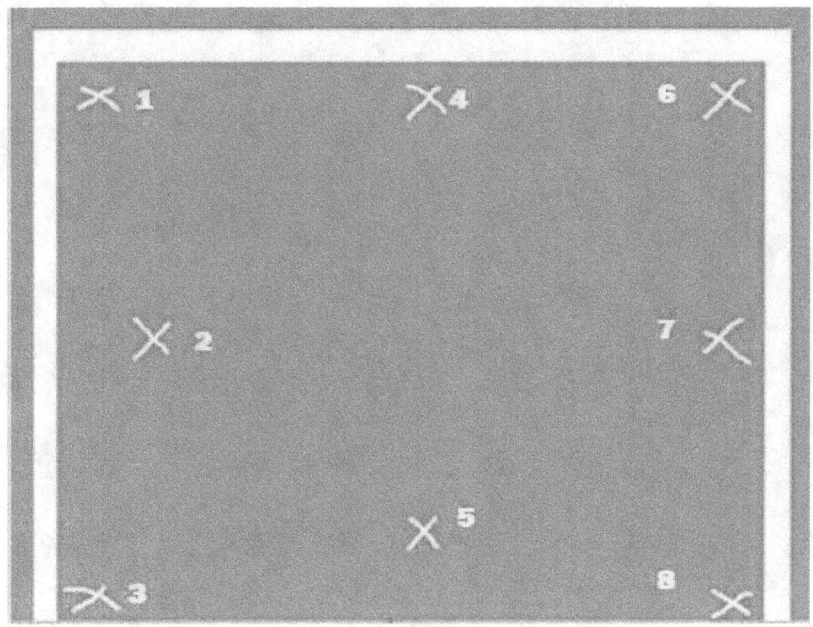

Date:

	Spot 1	Spot 2	Spot 3	Spot 4	Spot 5	Spot 6	Spot 7	Spot 8
Hit area and scored								
Hit area and saved								
Missed area								

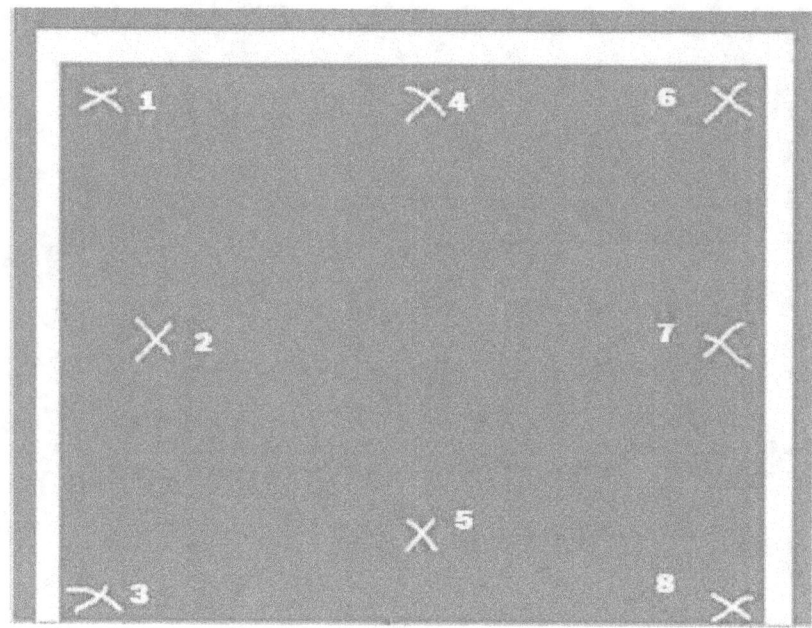

Date:

	Spot 1	Spot 2	Spot 3	Spot 4	Spot 5	Spot 6	Spot 7	Spot 8
Hit area and scored								
Hit area and saved								
Missed area								

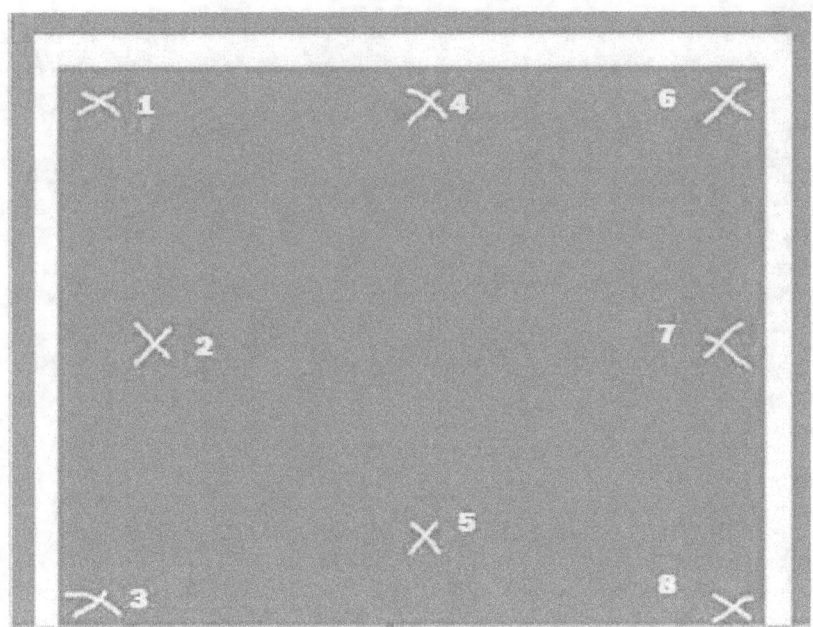

Date:

	Spot 1	Spot 2	Spot 3	Spot 4	Spot 5	Spot 6	Spot 7	Spot 8
Hit area and scored								
Hit area and saved								
Missed area								

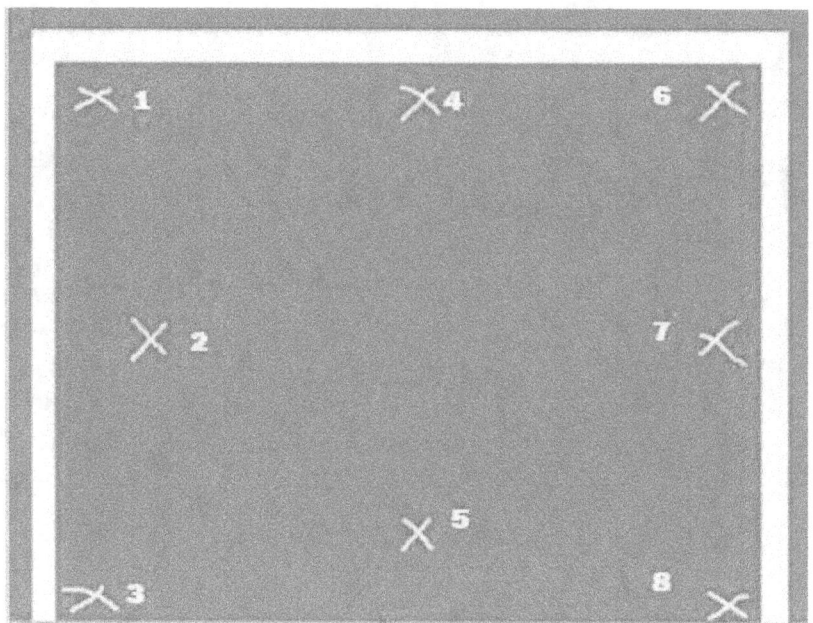

Date:

	Spot 1	Spot 2	Spot 3	Spot 4	Spot 5	Spot 6	Spot 7	Spot 8
Hit area and scored								
Hit area and saved								
Missed area								

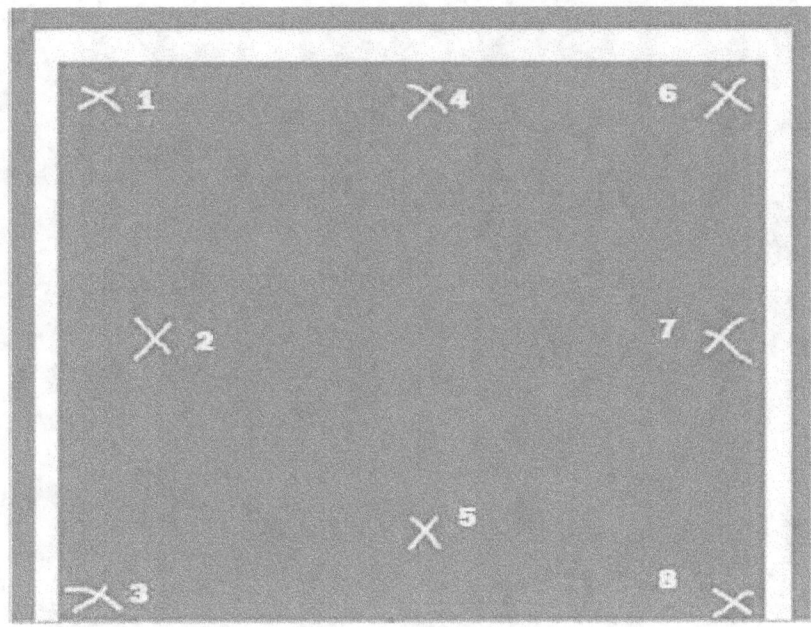

Date:

	Spot 1	Spot 2	Spot 3	Spot 4	Spot 5	Spot 6	Spot 7	Spot 8
Hit area and scored								
Hit area and saved								
Missed area								

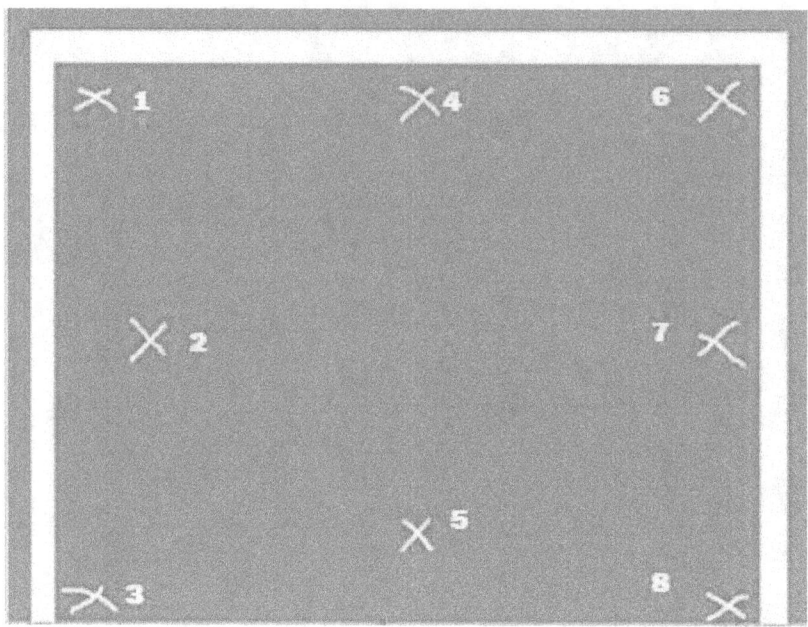

Date:

	Spot 1	Spot 2	Spot 3	Spot 4	Spot 5	Spot 6	Spot 7	Spot 8
Hit area and scored								
Hit area and saved								
Missed area								

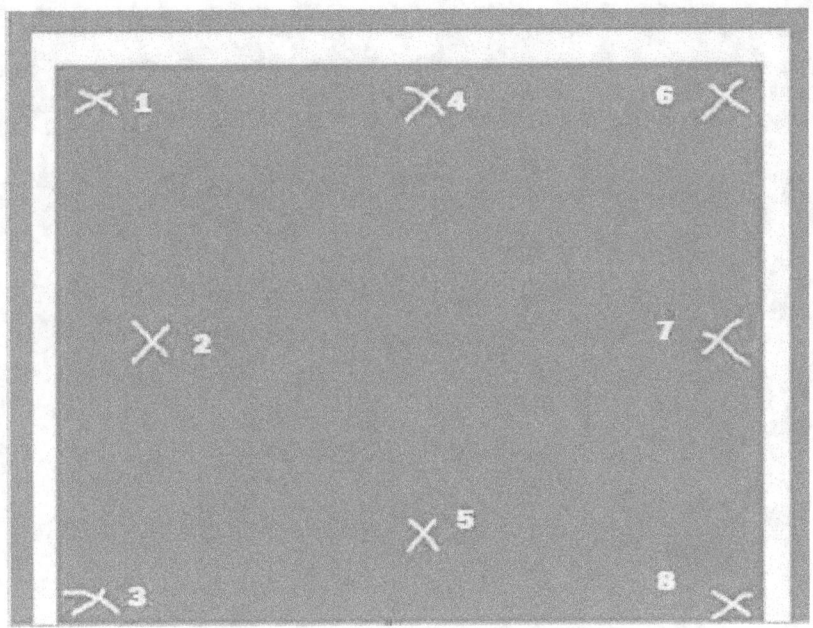

Date:

	Spot 1	Spot 2	Spot 3	Spot 4	Spot 5	Spot 6	Spot 7	Spot 8
Hit area and scored								
Hit area and saved								
Missed area								

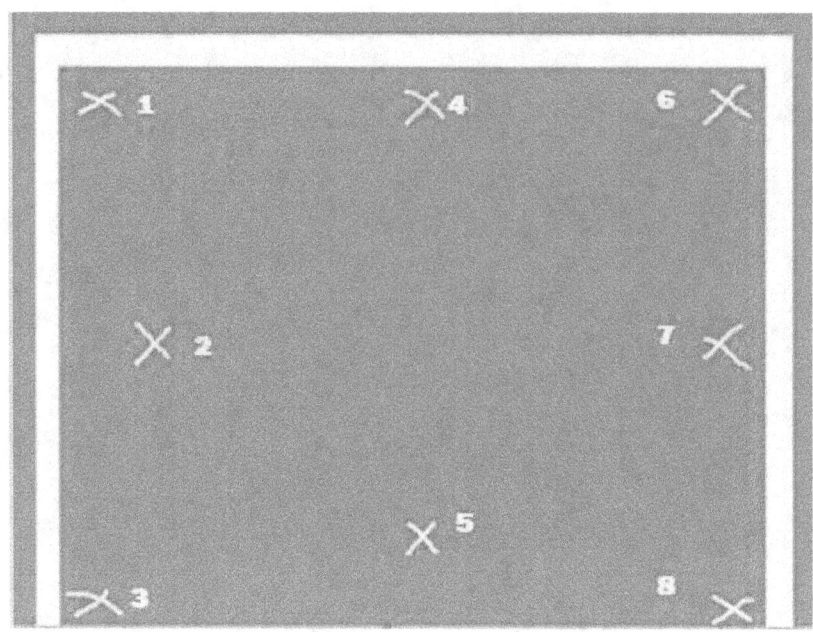

Date:

	Spot 1	Spot 2	Spot 3	Spot 4	Spot 5	Spot 6	Spot 7	Spot 8
Hit area and scored								
Hit area and saved								
Missed area								

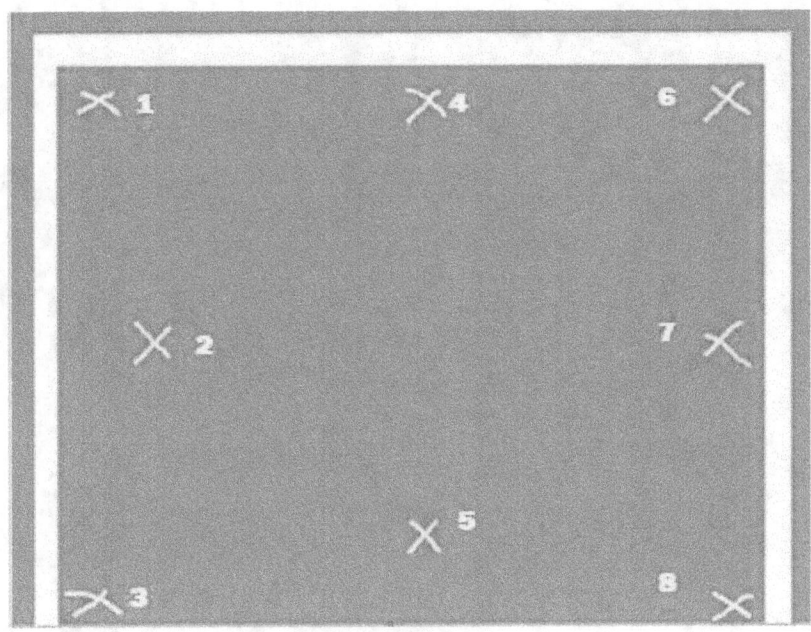

Date:

	Spot 1	Spot 2	Spot 3	Spot 4	Spot 5	Spot 6	Spot 7	Spot 8
Hit area and scored								
Hit area and saved								
Missed area								

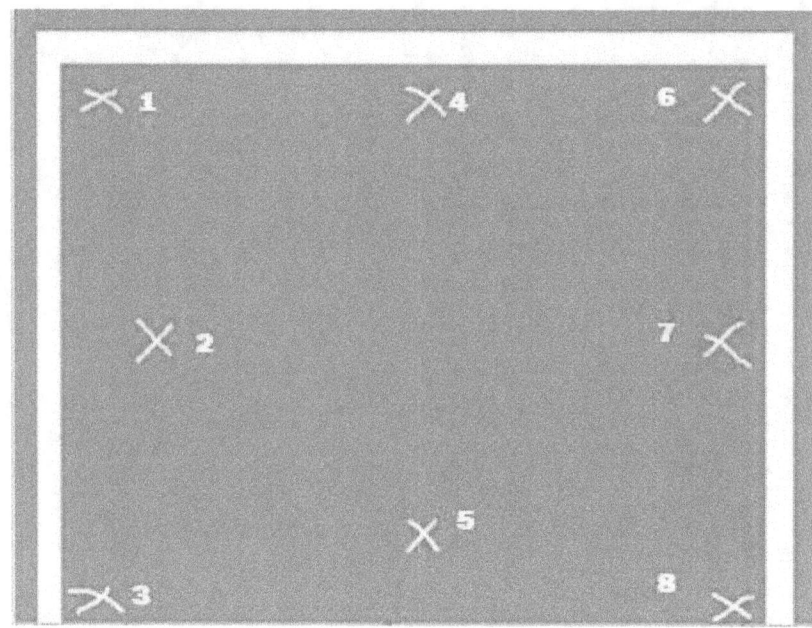

Date:

	Spot 1	Spot 2	Spot 3	Spot 4	Spot 5	Spot 6	Spot 7	Spot 8
Hit area and scored								
Hit area and saved								
Missed area								

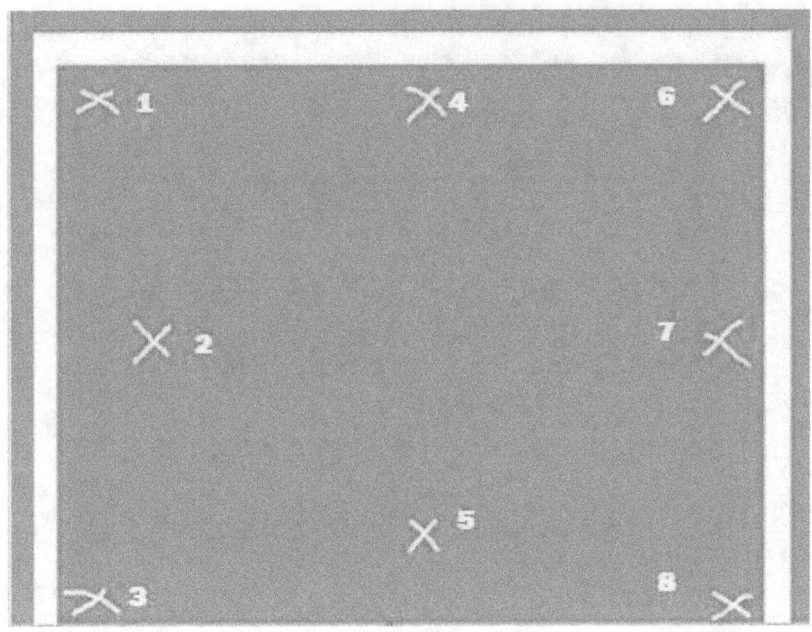

Date:

	Spot 1	Spot 2	Spot 3	Spot 4	Spot 5	Spot 6	Spot 7	Spot 8
Hit area and scored								
Hit area and saved								
Missed area								

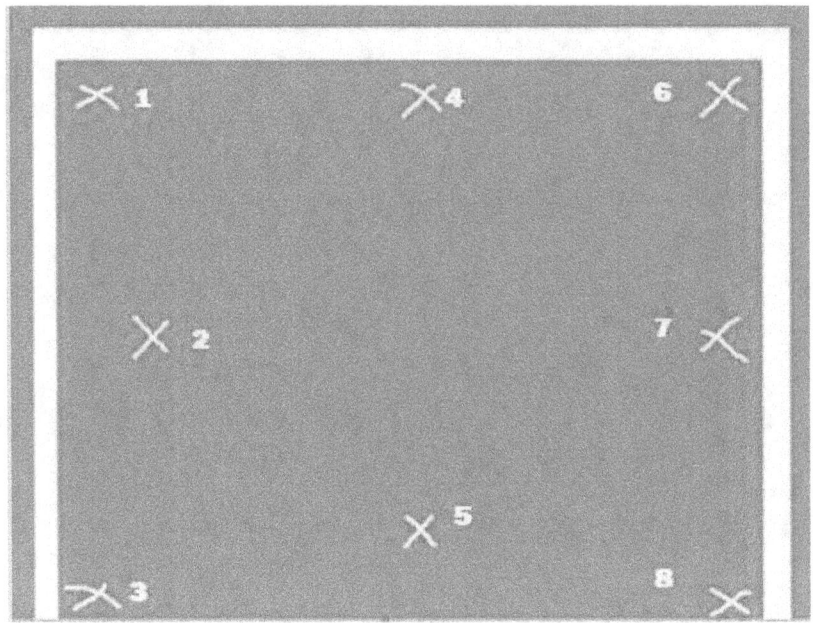

Date:

	Spot 1	Spot 2	Spot 3	Spot 4	Spot 5	Spot 6	Spot 7	Spot 8
Hit area and scored								
Hit area and saved								
Missed area								

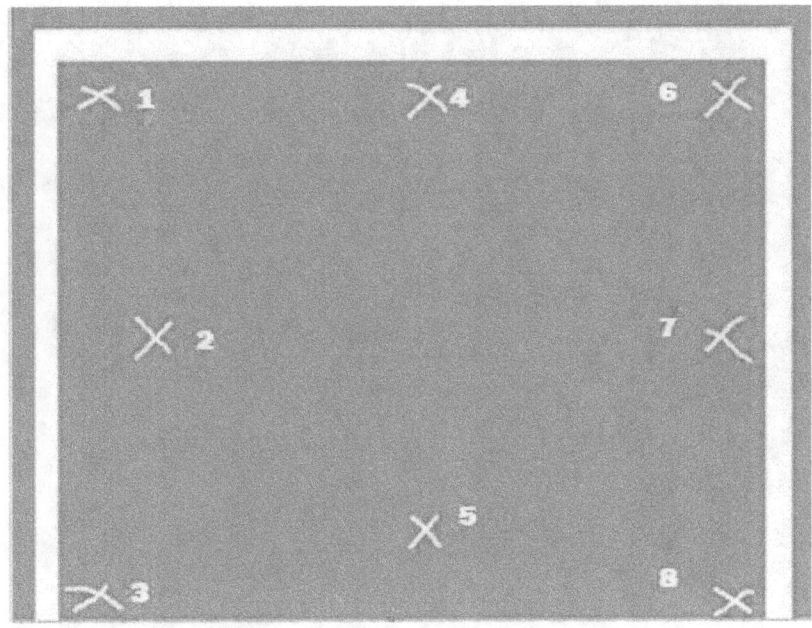

Date:

	Spot 1	Spot 2	Spot 3	Spot 4	Spot 5	Spot 6	Spot 7	Spot 8
Hit area and scored								
Hit area and saved								
Missed area								

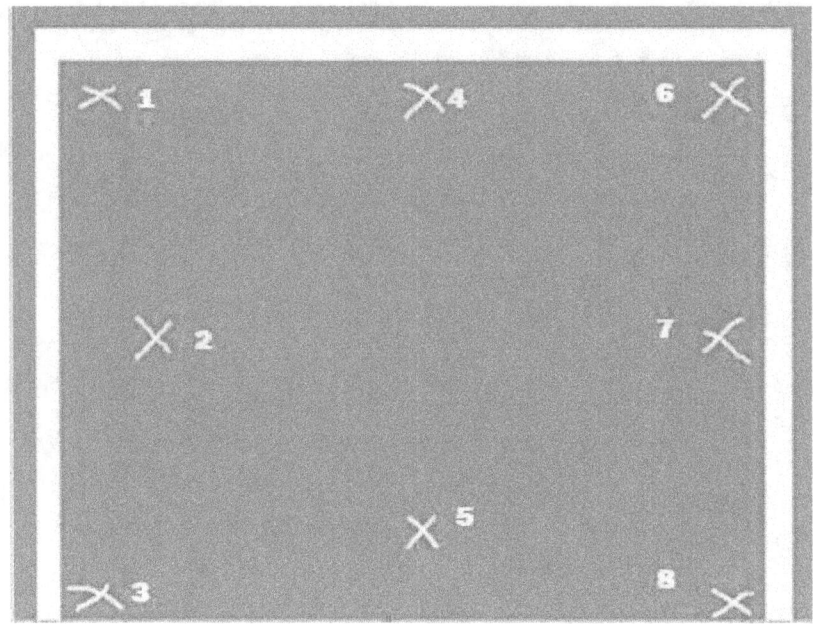

Date:

	Spot 1	Spot 2	Spot 3	Spot 4	Spot 5	Spot 6	Spot 7	Spot 8
Hit area and scored								
Hit area and saved								
Missed area								

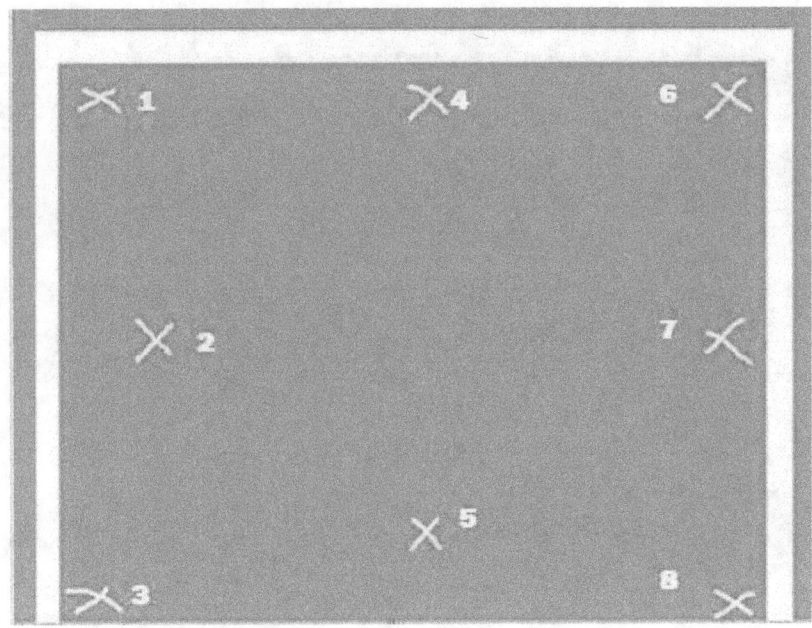

Date:

	Spot 1	Spot 2	Spot 3	Spot 4	Spot 5	Spot 6	Spot 7	Spot 8
Hit area and scored								
Hit area and saved								
Missed area								

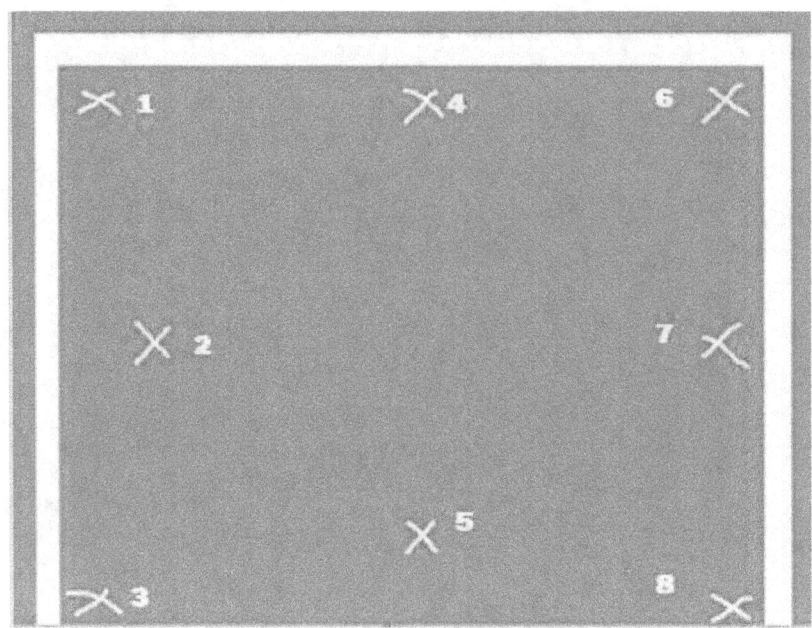

Date:

	Spot 1	Spot 2	Spot 3	Spot 4	Spot 5	Spot 6	Spot 7	Spot 8
Hit area and scored								
Hit area and saved								
Missed area								

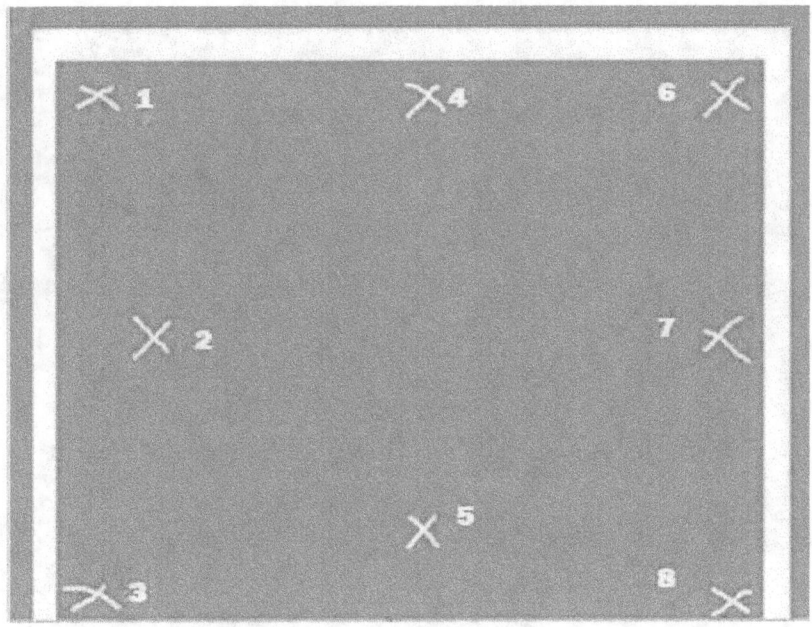

Date:

	Spot 1	Spot 2	Spot 3	Spot 4	Spot 5	Spot 6	Spot 7	Spot 8
Hit area and scored								
Hit area and saved								
Missed area								

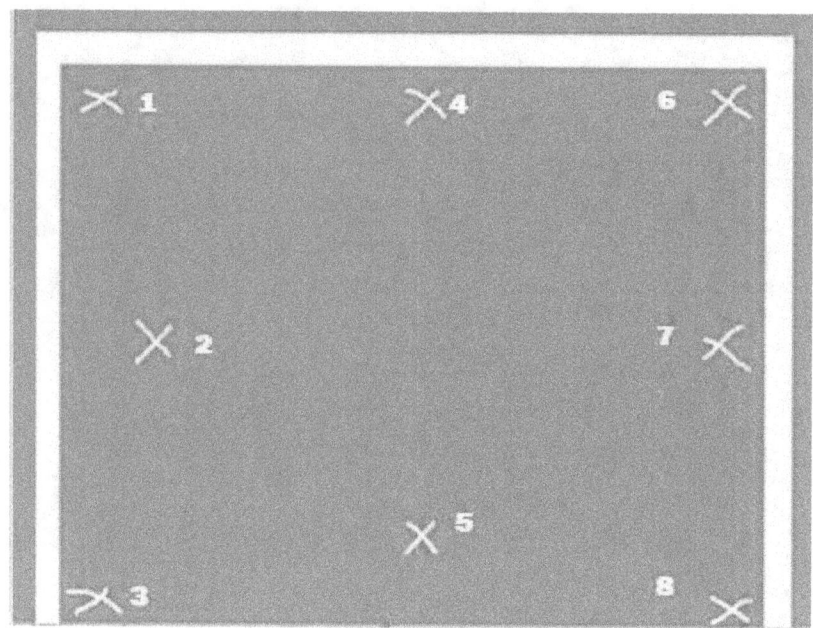

Date:

	Spot 1	Spot 2	Spot 3	Spot 4	Spot 5	Spot 6	Spot 7	Spot 8
Hit area and scored								
Hit area and saved								
Missed area								

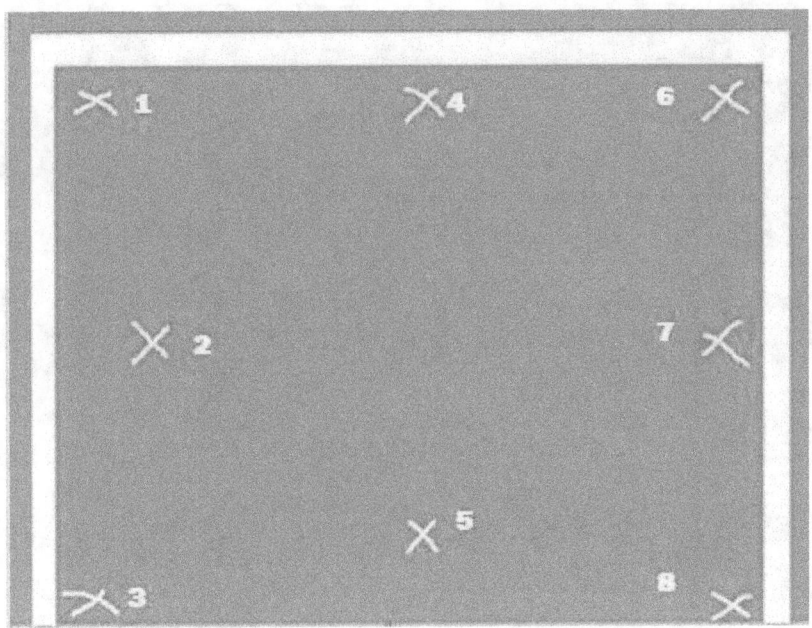

Date:

	Spot 1	Spot 2	Spot 3	Spot 4	Spot 5	Spot 6	Spot 7	Spot 8
Hit area and scored								
Hit area and saved								
Missed area								

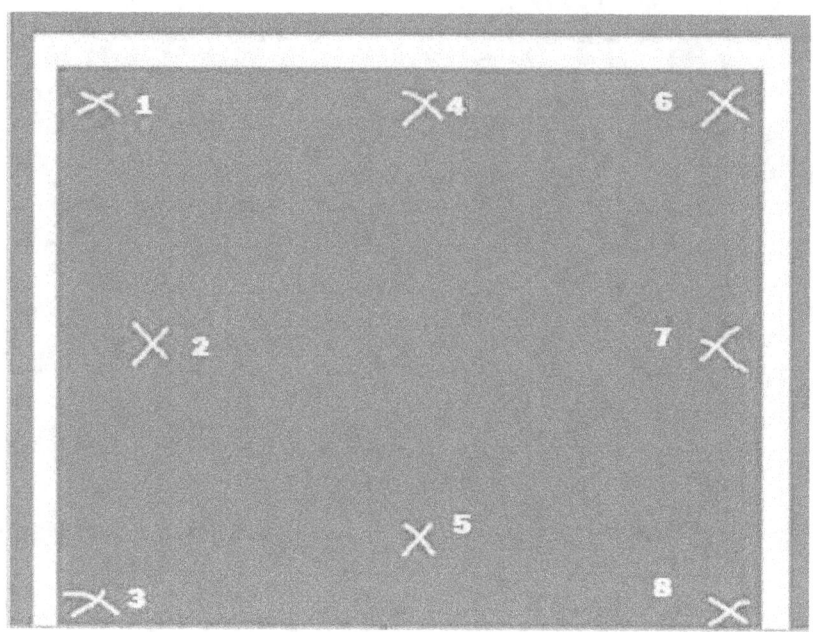

Date:

	Spot 1	Spot 2	Spot 3	Spot 4	Spot 5	Spot 6	Spot 7	Spot 8
Hit area and scored								
Hit area and saved								
Missed area								

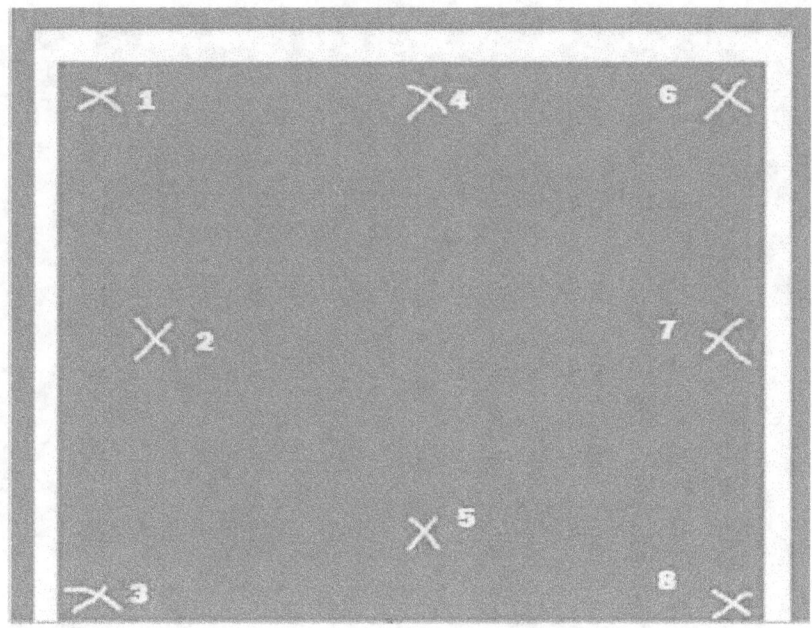

Date:

	Spot 1	Spot 2	Spot 3	Spot 4	Spot 5	Spot 6	Spot 7	Spot 8
Hit area and scored								
Hit area and saved								
Missed area								

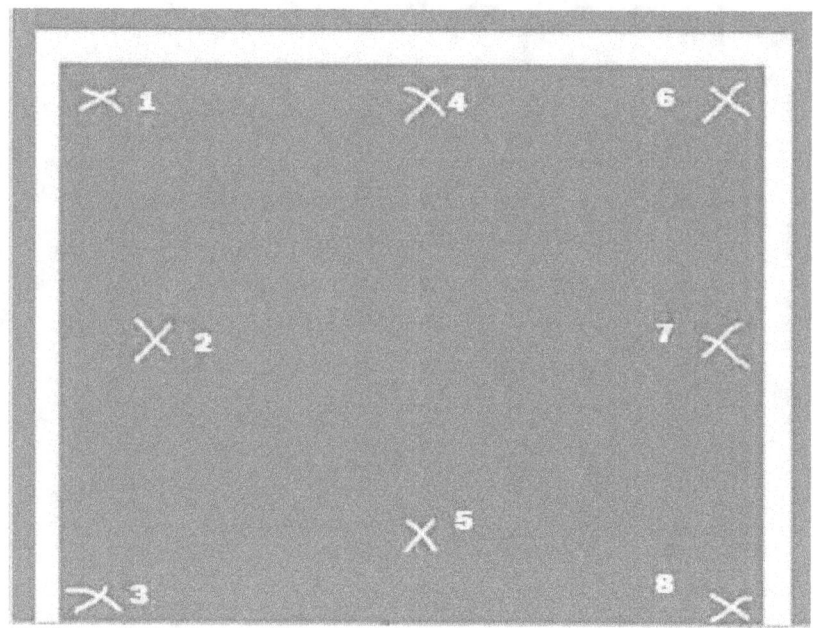

Date:

	Spot 1	Spot 2	Spot 3	Spot 4	Spot 5	Spot 6	Spot 7	Spot 8
Hit area and scored								
Hit area and saved								
Missed area								

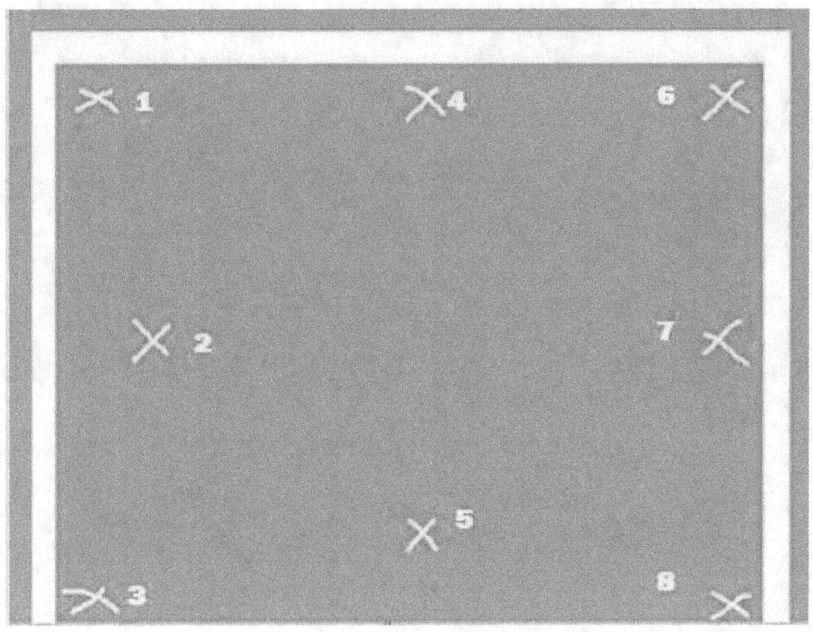

Date:

	Spot 1	Spot 2	Spot 3	Spot 4	Spot 5	Spot 6	Spot 7	Spot 8
Hit area and scored								
Hit area and saved								
Missed area								

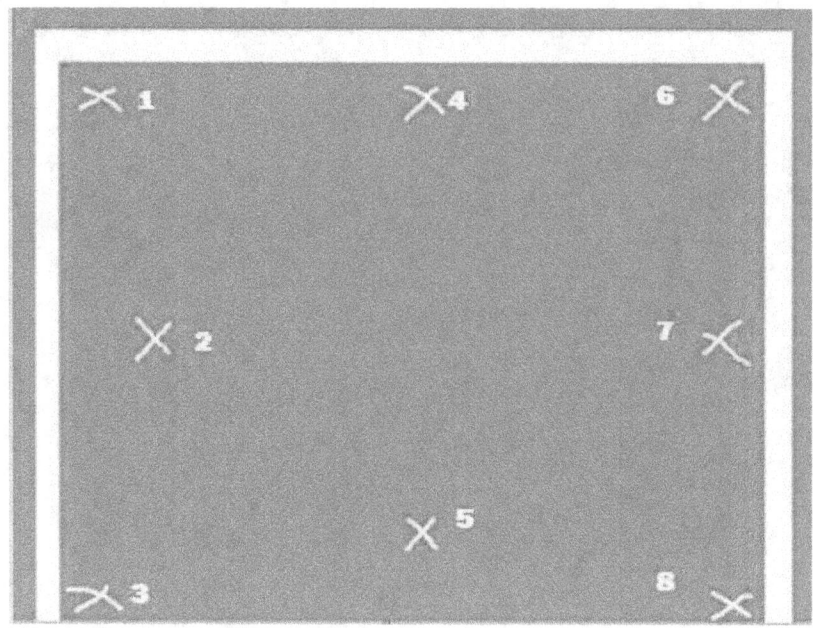

Date:

	Spot 1	Spot 2	Spot 3	Spot 4	Spot 5	Spot 6	Spot 7	Spot 8
Hit area and scored								
Hit area and saved								
Missed area								

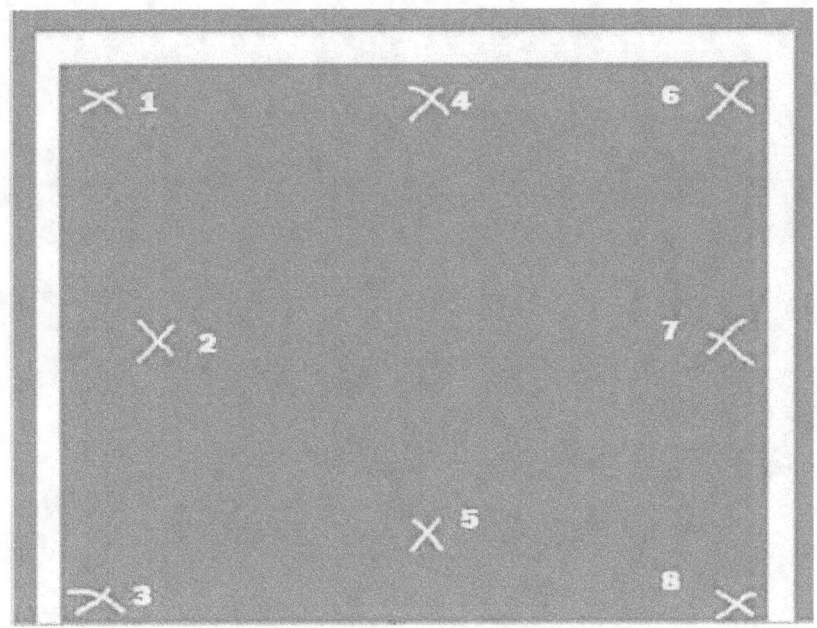

Date:

	Spot 1	Spot 2	Spot 3	Spot 4	Spot 5	Spot 6	Spot 7	Spot 8
Hit area and scored								
Hit area and saved								
Missed area								

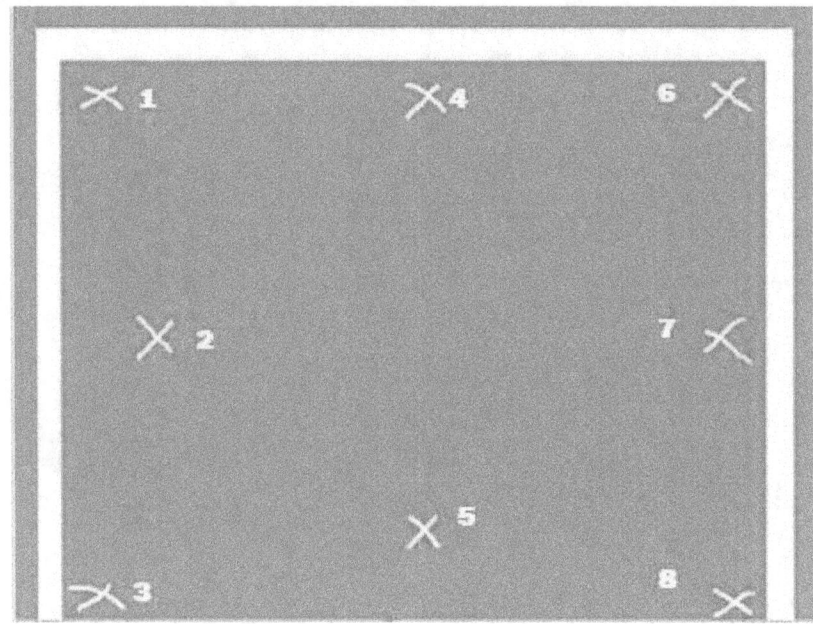

Date:

	Spot 1	Spot 2	Spot 3	Spot 4	Spot 5	Spot 6	Spot 7	Spot 8
Hit area and scored								
Hit area and saved								
Missed area								

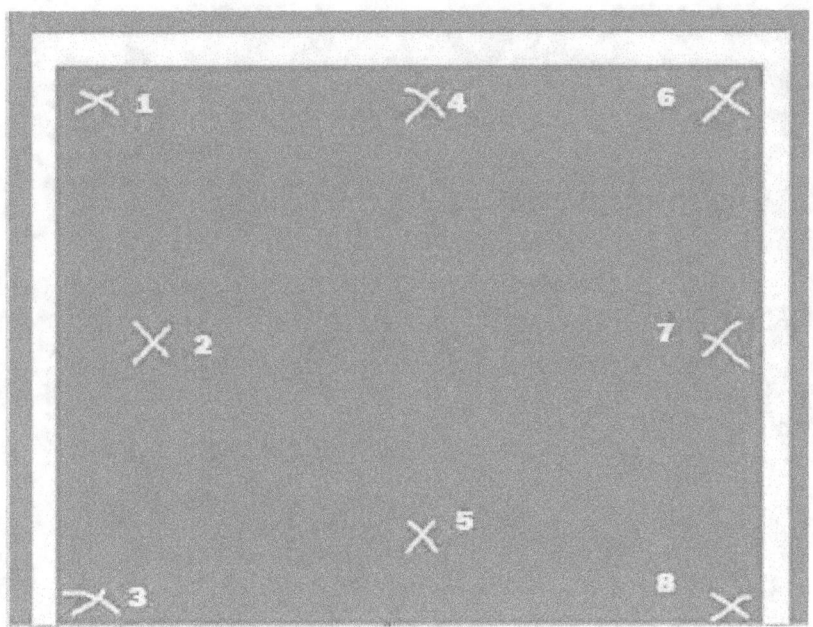

Date:

	Spot 1	Spot 2	Spot 3	Spot 4	Spot 5	Spot 6	Spot 7	Spot 8
Hit area and scored								
Hit area and saved								
Missed area								

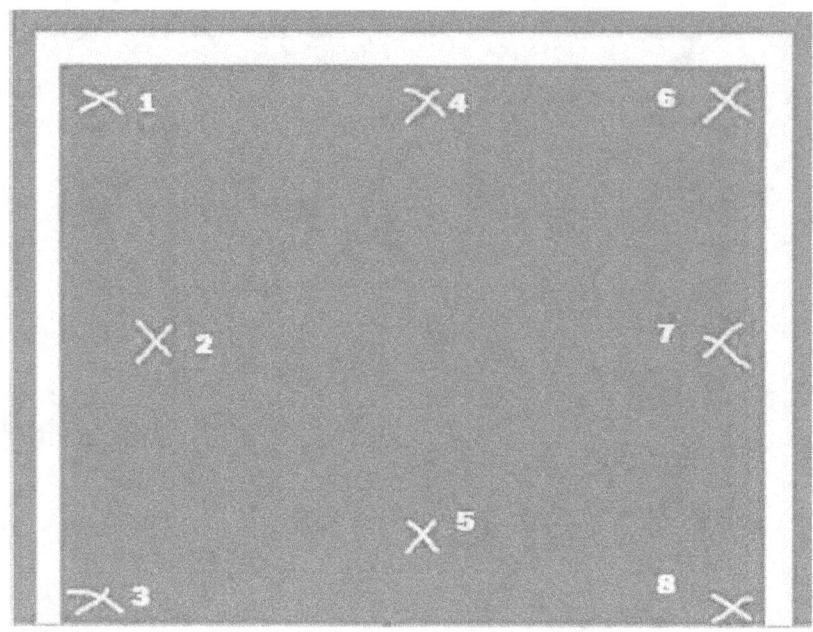

Date:

	Spot 1	Spot 2	Spot 3	Spot 4	Spot 5	Spot 6	Spot 7	Spot 8
Hit area and scored								
Hit area and saved								
Missed area								

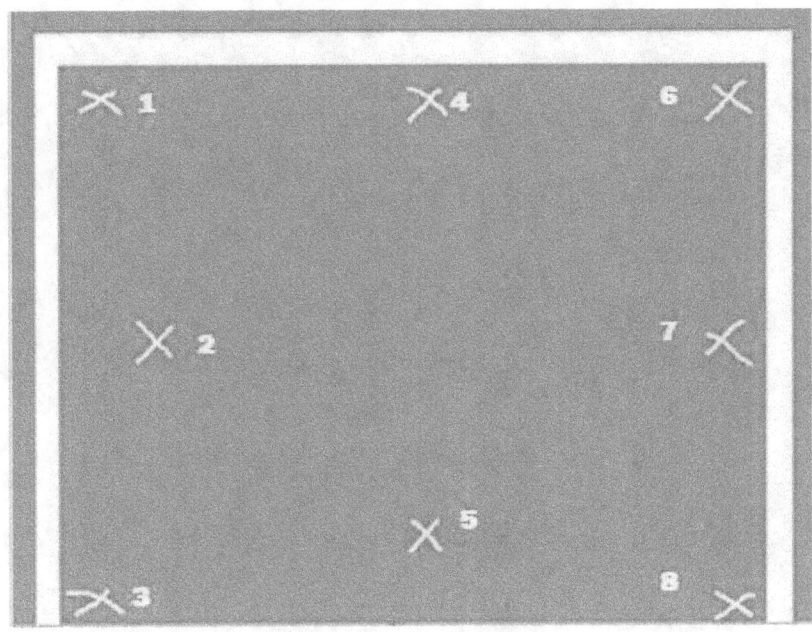

Date:

	Spot 1	Spot 2	Spot 3	Spot 4	Spot 5	Spot 6	Spot 7	Spot 8
Hit area and scored								
Hit area and saved								
Missed area								

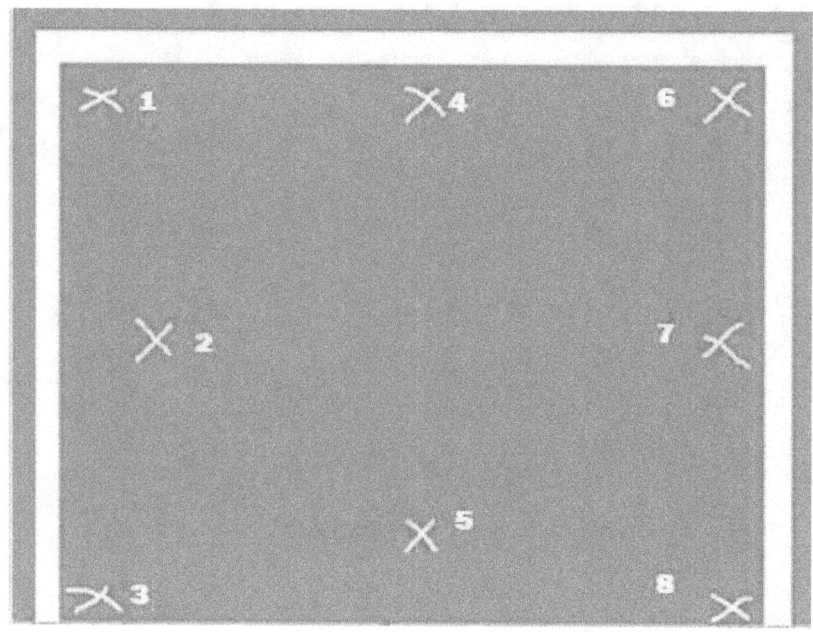

Date:

	Spot 1	Spot 2	Spot 3	Spot 4	Spot 5	Spot 6	Spot 7	Spot 8
Hit area and scored								
Hit area and saved								
Missed area								

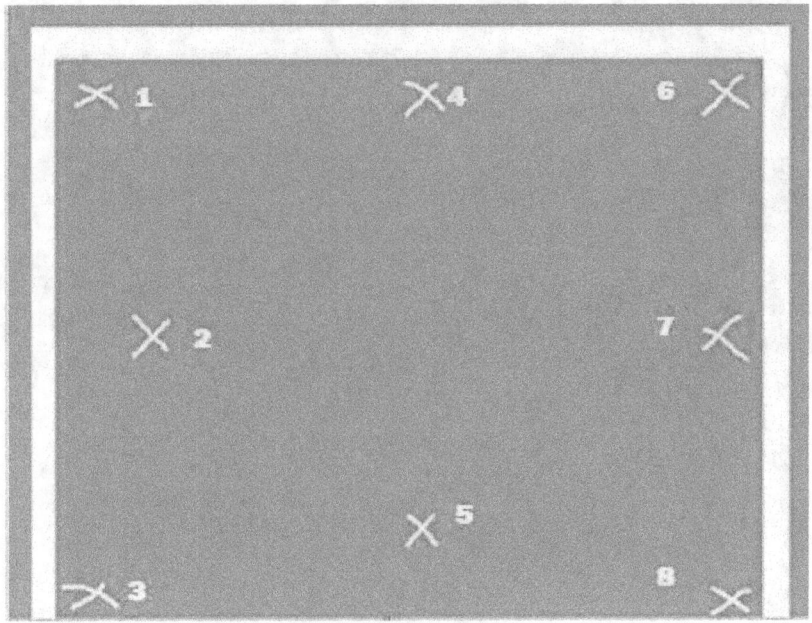

Date:

	Spot 1	Spot 2	Spot 3	Spot 4	Spot 5	Spot 6	Spot 7	Spot 8
Hit area and scored								
Hit area and saved								
Missed area								

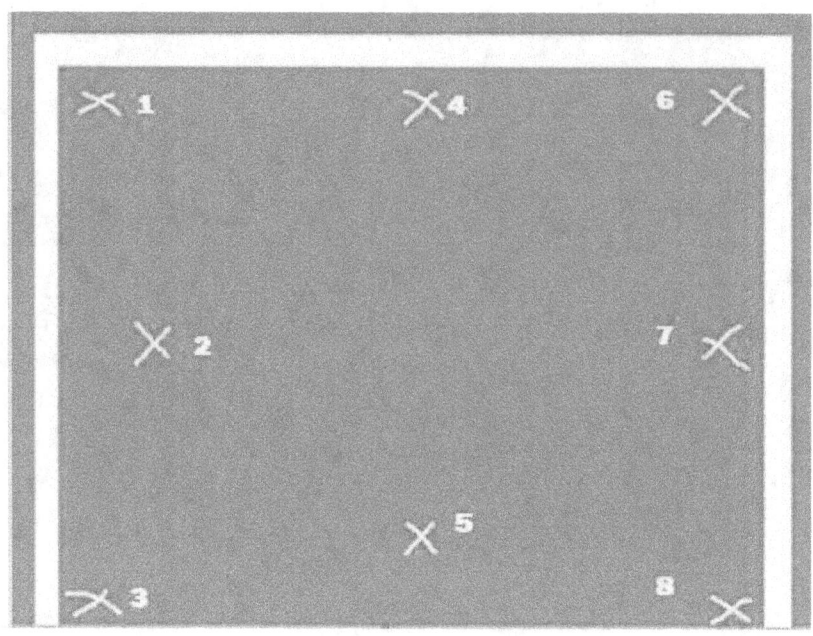

Date:

	Spot 1	Spot 2	Spot 3	Spot 4	Spot 5	Spot 6	Spot 7	Spot 8
Hit area and scored								
Hit area and saved								
Missed area								

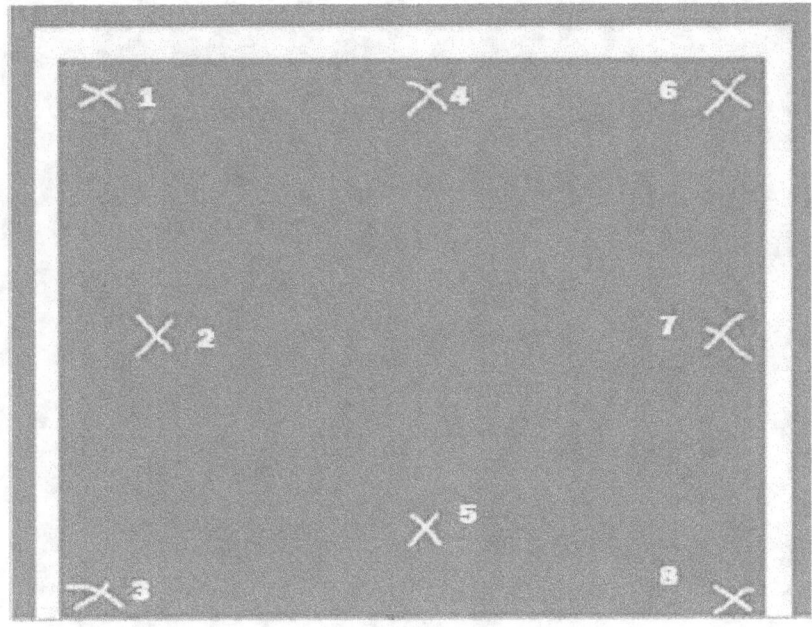

Date:

	Spot 1	Spot 2	Spot 3	Spot 4	Spot 5	Spot 6	Spot 7	Spot 8
Hit area and scored								
Hit area and saved								
Missed area								

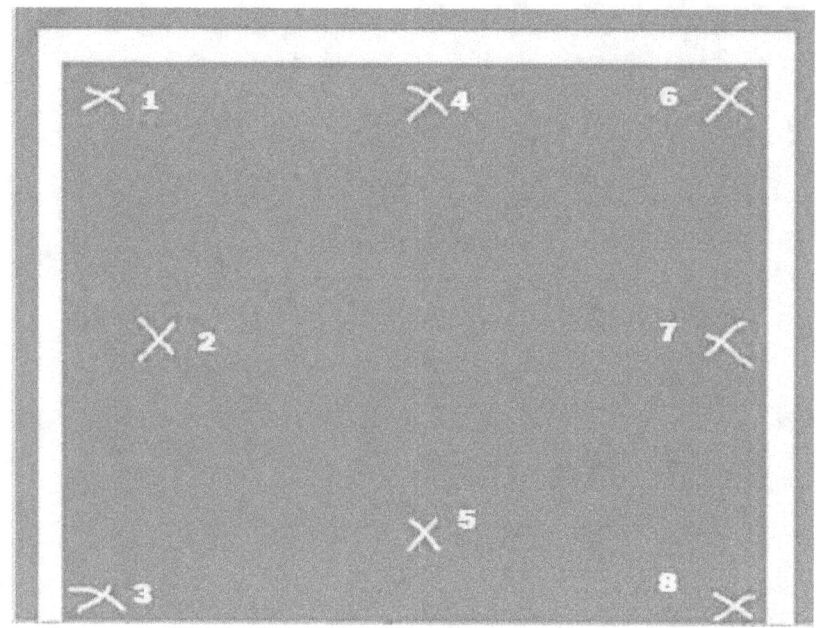

Date:

	Spot 1	Spot 2	Spot 3	Spot 4	Spot 5	Spot 6	Spot 7	Spot 8
Hit area and scored								
Hit area and saved								
Missed area								

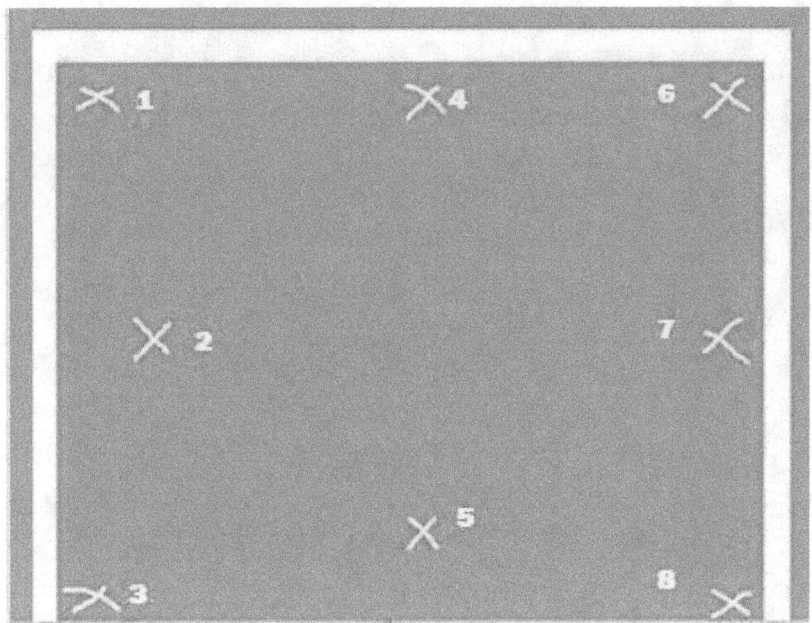

Date:

	Spot 1	Spot 2	Spot 3	Spot 4	Spot 5	Spot 6	Spot 7	Spot 8
Hit area and scored								
Hit area and saved								
Missed area								

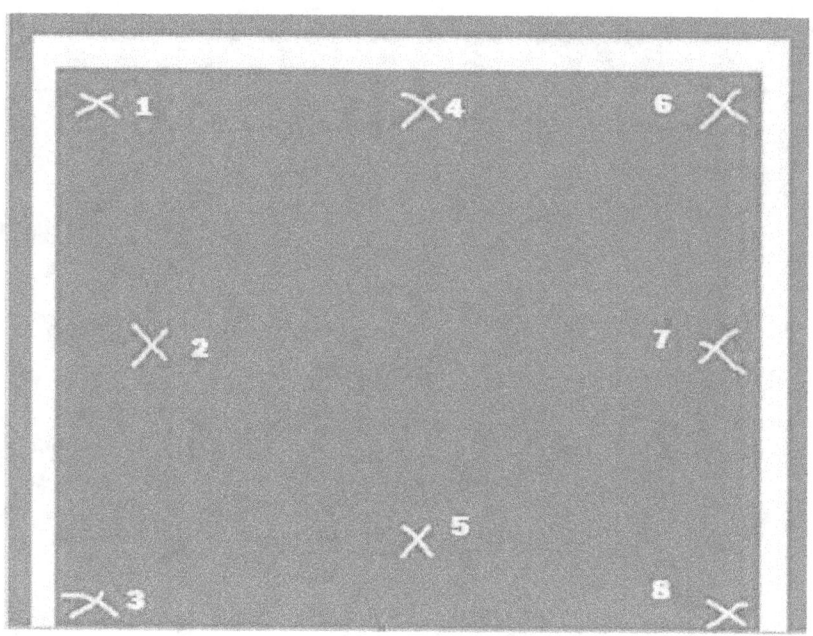

Date:

	Spot 1	Spot 2	Spot 3	Spot 4	Spot 5	Spot 6	Spot 7	Spot 8
Hit area and scored								
Hit area and saved								
Missed area								

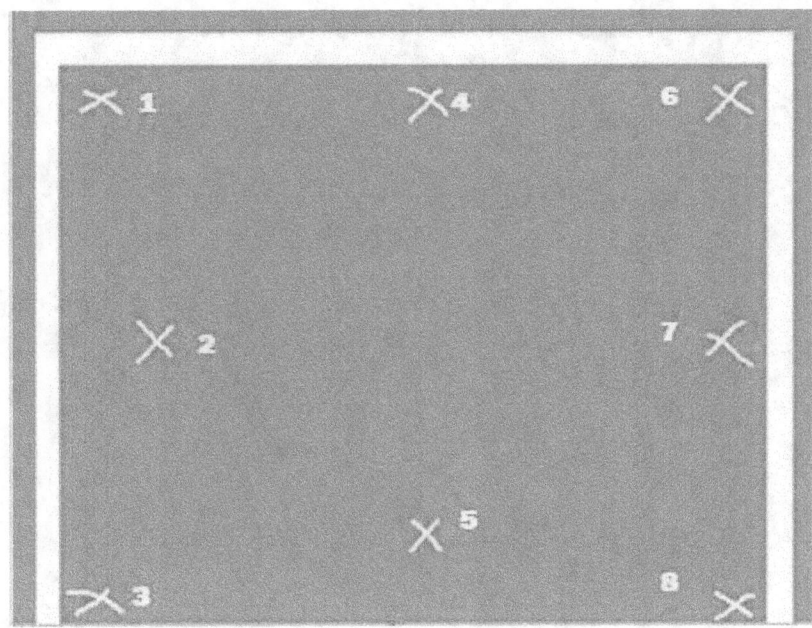

Date:

	Spot 1	Spot 2	Spot 3	Spot 4	Spot 5	Spot 6	Spot 7	Spot 8
Hit area and scored								
Hit area and saved								
Missed area								

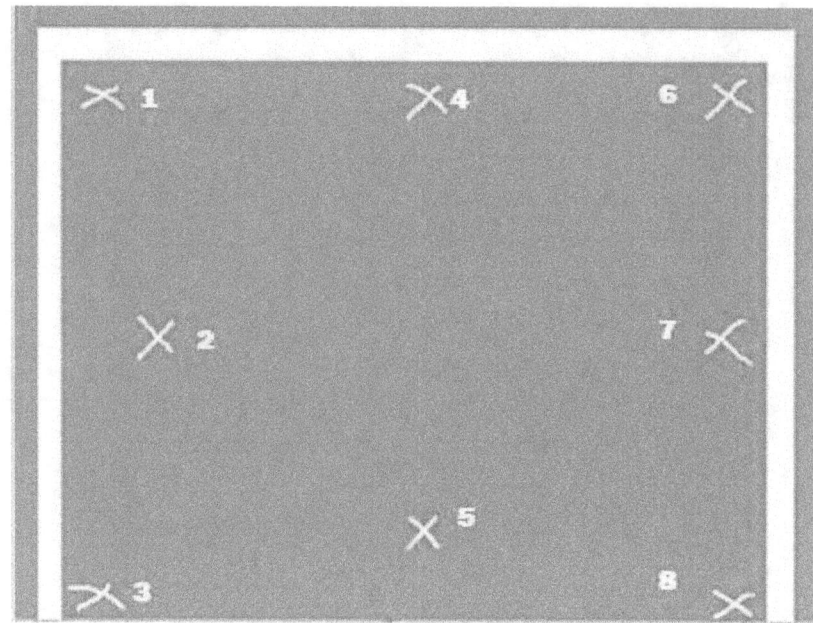

Date:

	Spot 1	Spot 2	Spot 3	Spot 4	Spot 5	Spot 6	Spot 7	Spot 8
Hit area and scored								
Hit area and saved								
Missed area								

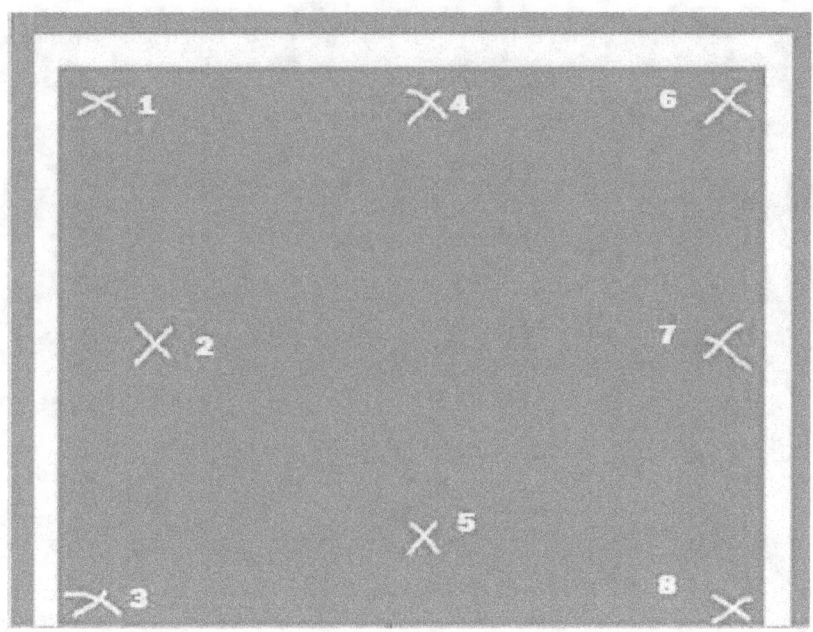

Date:

	Spot 1	Spot 2	Spot 3	Spot 4	Spot 5	Spot 6	Spot 7	Spot 8
Hit area and scored								
Hit area and saved								
Missed area								

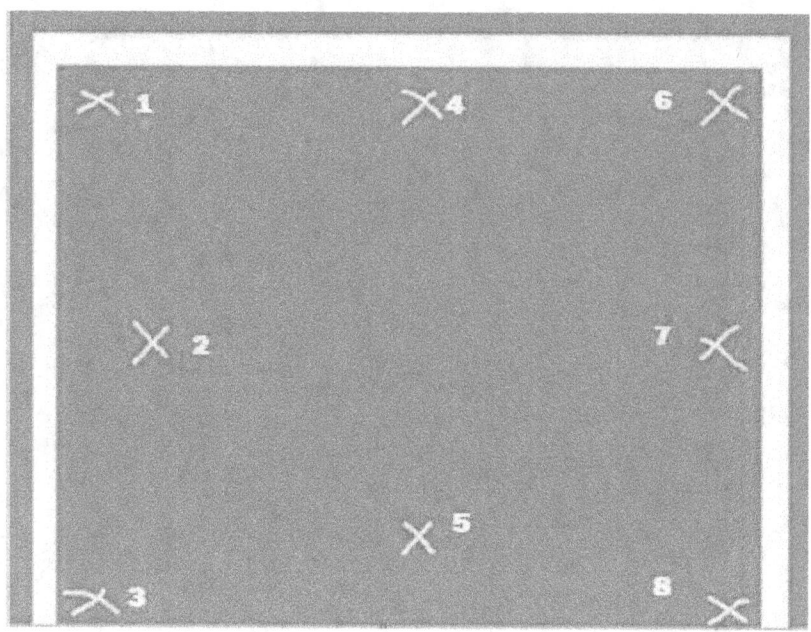

Date:

	Spot 1	Spot 2	Spot 3	Spot 4	Spot 5	Spot 6	Spot 7	Spot 8
Hit area and scored								
Hit area and saved								
Missed area								

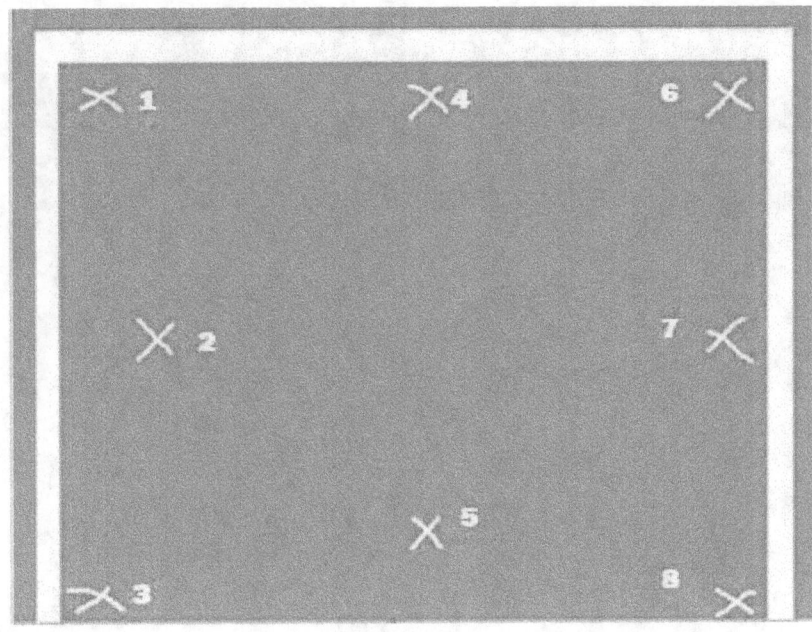

Date:

	Spot 1	Spot 2	Spot 3	Spot 4	Spot 5	Spot 6	Spot 7	Spot 8
Hit area and scored								
Hit area and saved								
Missed area								

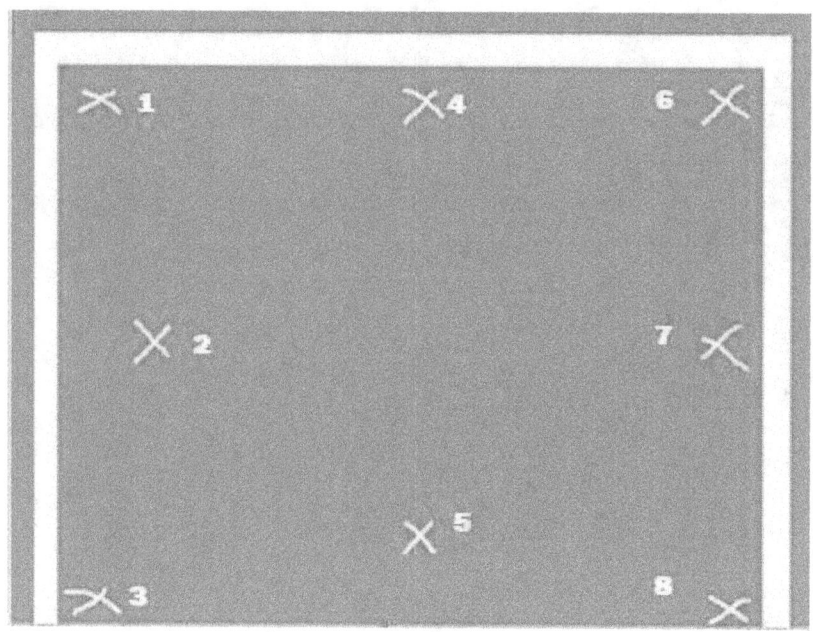

Date:

	Spot 1	Spot 2	Spot 3	Spot 4	Spot 5	Spot 6	Spot 7	Spot 8
Hit area and scored								
Hit area and saved								
Missed area								

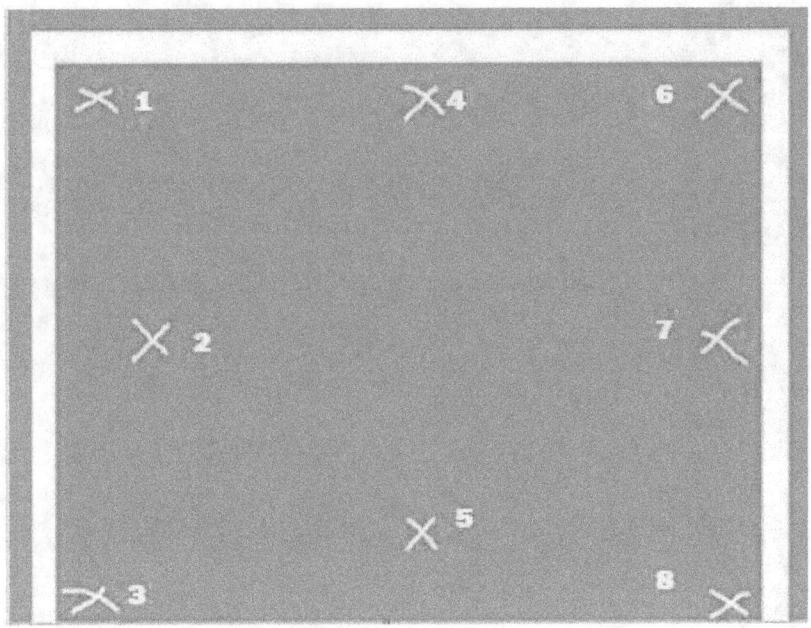

Date:

	Spot 1	Spot 2	Spot 3	Spot 4	Spot 5	Spot 6	Spot 7	Spot 8
Hit area and scored								
Hit area and saved								
Missed area								

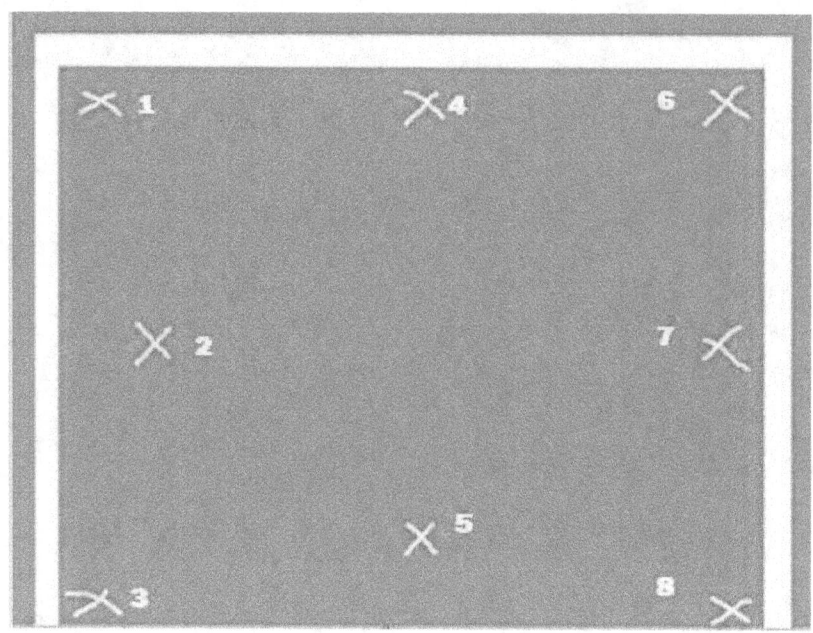

Date:

	Spot 1	Spot 2	Spot 3	Spot 4	Spot 5	Spot 6	Spot 7	Spot 8
Hit area and scored								
Hit area and saved								
Missed area								

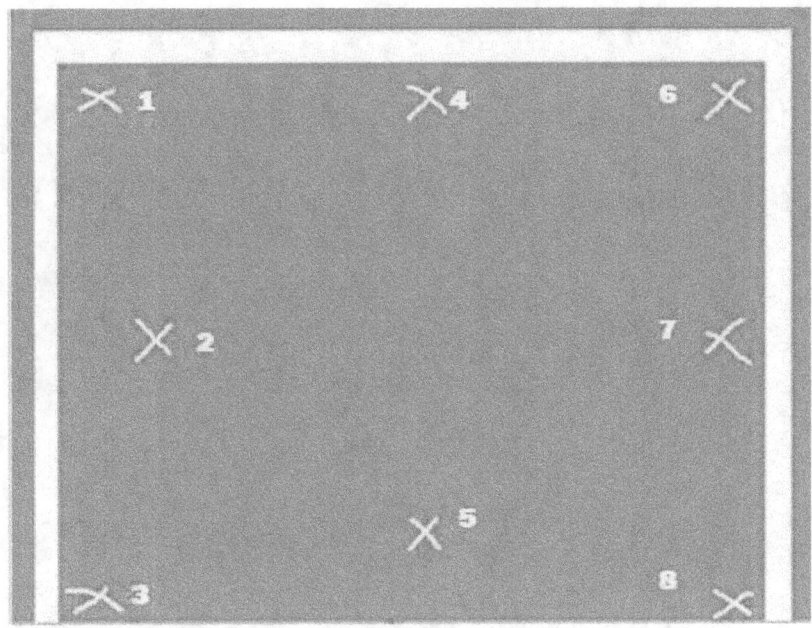

Date:

	Spot 1	Spot 2	Spot 3	Spot 4	Spot 5	Spot 6	Spot 7	Spot 8
Hit area and scored								
Hit area and saved								
Missed area								

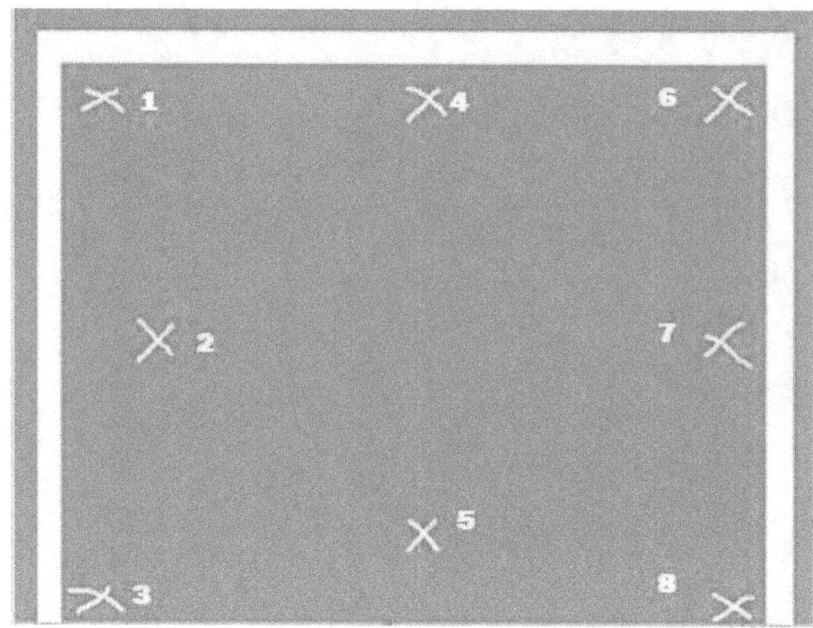

Date:

	Spot 1	Spot 2	Spot 3	Spot 4	Spot 5	Spot 6	Spot 7	Spot 8
Hit area and scored								
Hit area and saved								
Missed area								

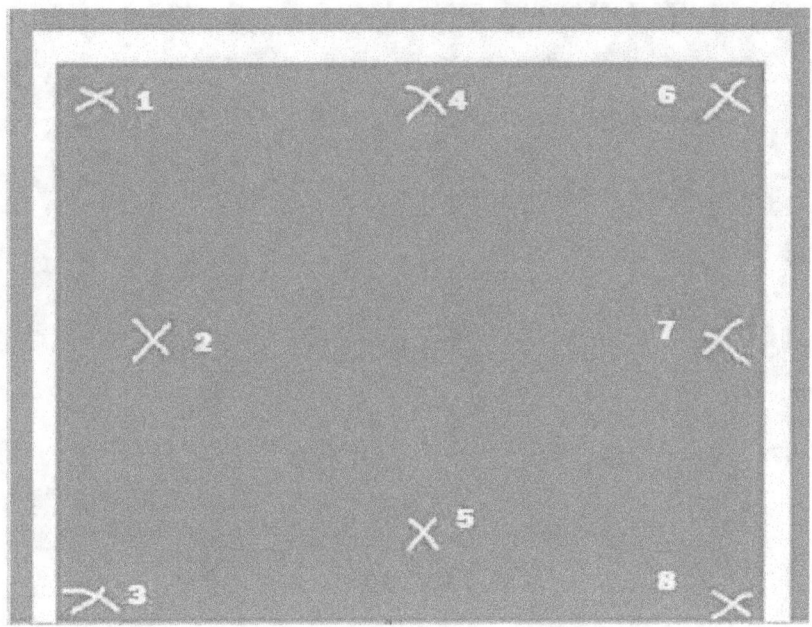

Date:

	Spot 1	Spot 2	Spot 3	Spot 4	Spot 5	Spot 6	Spot 7	Spot 8
Hit area and scored								
Hit area and saved								
Missed area								

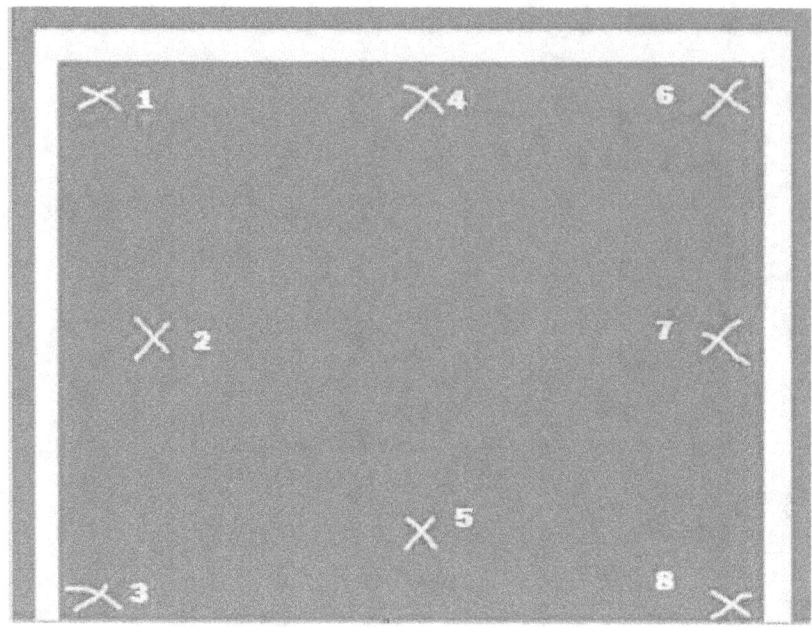

Date:

	Spot 1	Spot 2	Spot 3	Spot 4	Spot 5	Spot 6	Spot 7	Spot 8
Hit area and scored								
Hit area and saved								
Missed area								

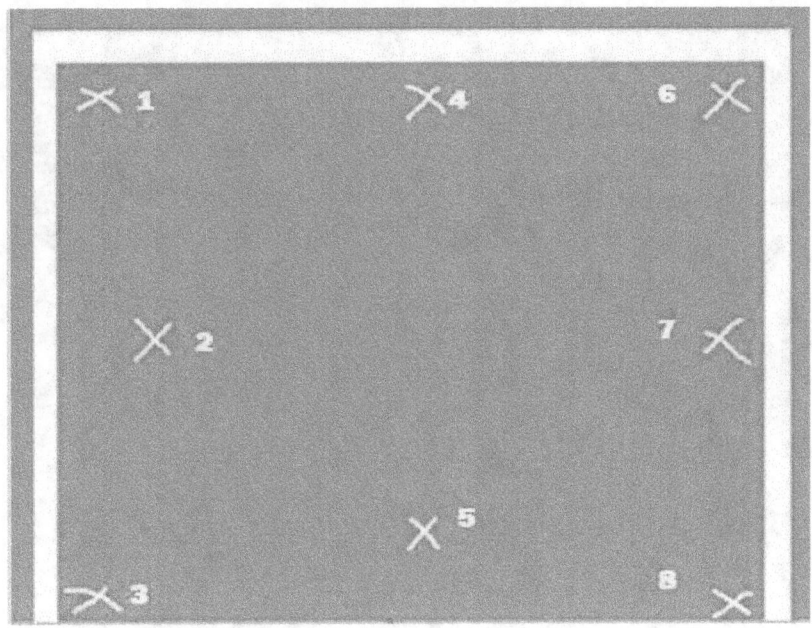

Date:

	Spot 1	Spot 2	Spot 3	Spot 4	Spot 5	Spot 6	Spot 7	Spot 8
Hit area and scored								
Hit area and saved								
Missed area								

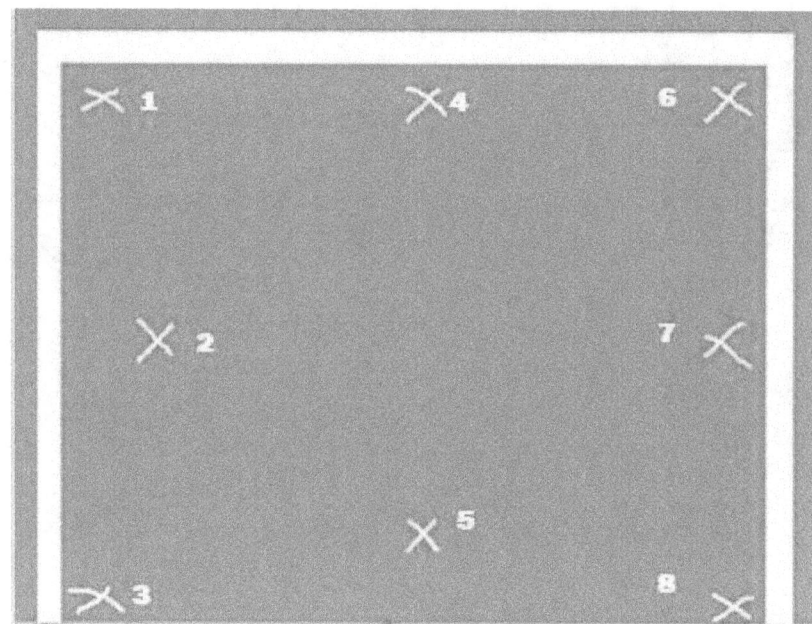

Date:

	Spot 1	Spot 2	Spot 3	Spot 4	Spot 5	Spot 6	Spot 7	Spot 8
Hit area and scored								
Hit area and saved								
Missed area								

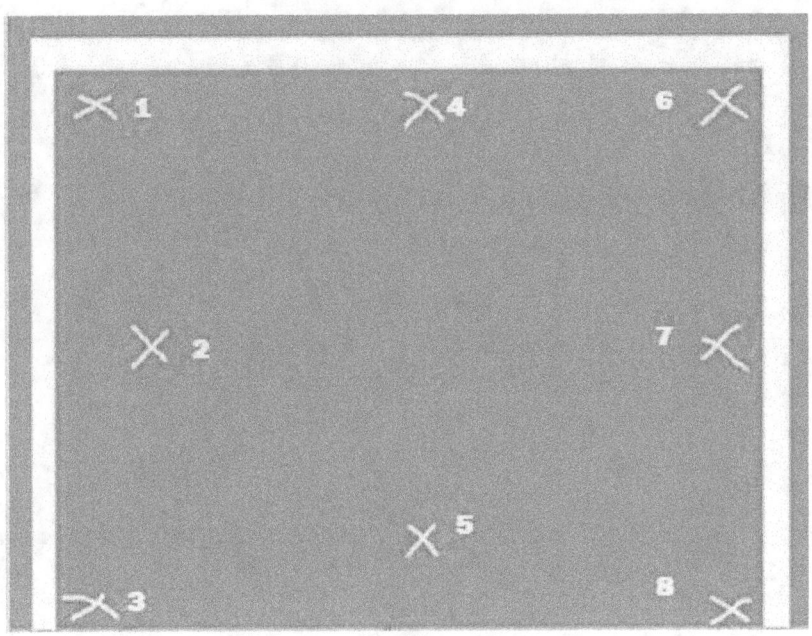

Date:

	Spot 1	Spot 2	Spot 3	Spot 4	Spot 5	Spot 6	Spot 7	Spot 8
Hit area and scored								
Hit area and saved								
Missed area								

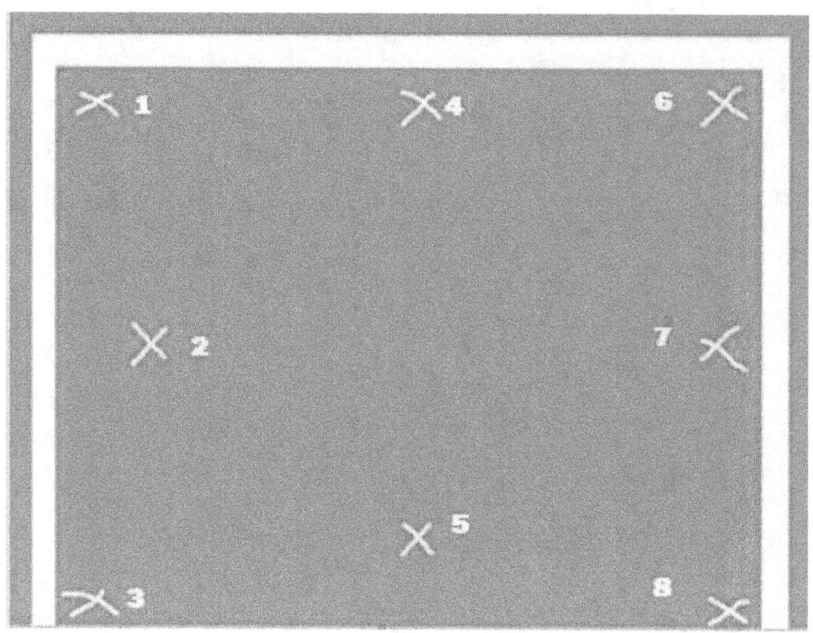

Date:

	Spot 1	Spot 2	Spot 3	Spot 4	Spot 5	Spot 6	Spot 7	Spot 8
Hit area and scored								
Hit area and saved								
Missed area								

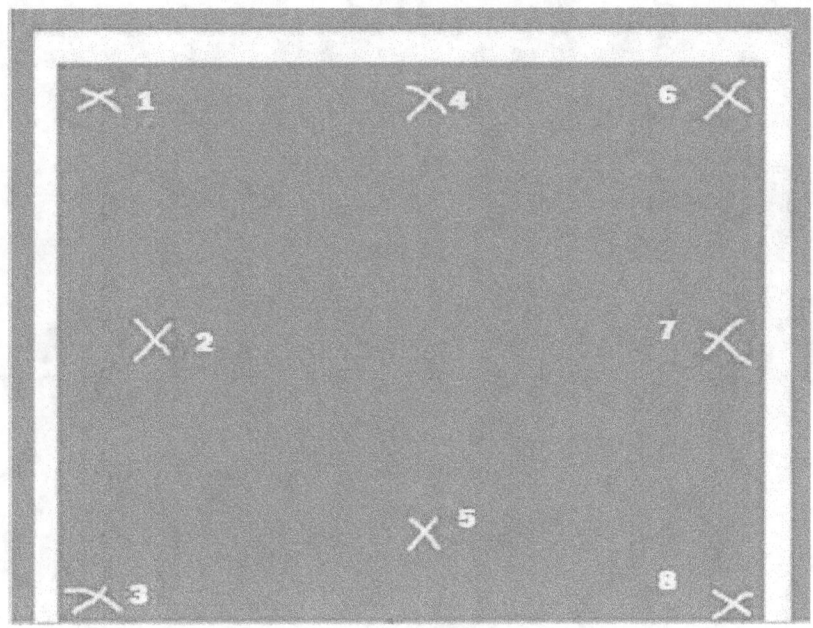

Date:

	Spot 1	Spot 2	Spot 3	Spot 4	Spot 5	Spot 6	Spot 7	Spot 8
Hit area and scored								
Hit area and saved								
Missed area								

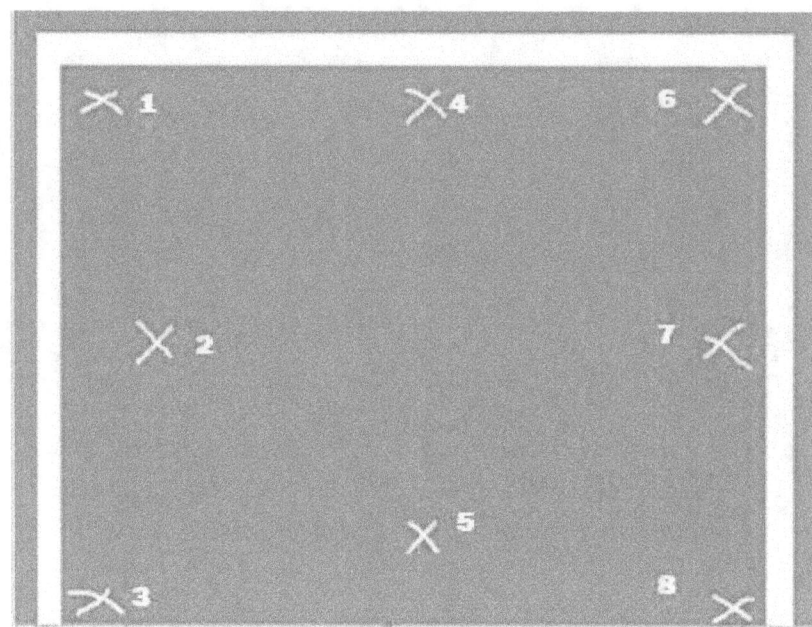

Date:

	Spot 1	Spot 2	Spot 3	Spot 4	Spot 5	Spot 6	Spot 7	Spot 8
Hit area and scored								
Hit area and saved								
Missed area								

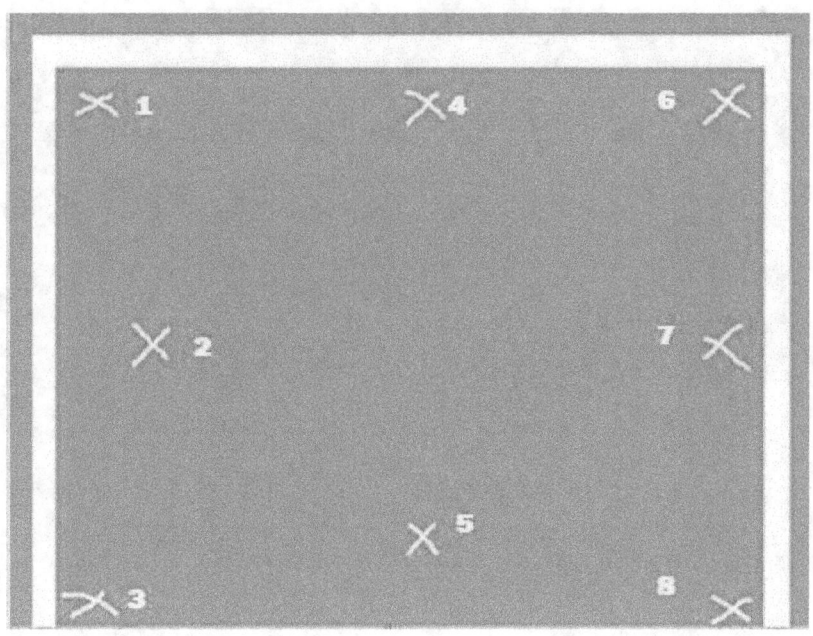

Date:

	Spot 1	Spot 2	Spot 3	Spot 4	Spot 5	Spot 6	Spot 7	Spot 8
Hit area and scored								
Hit area and saved								
Missed area								

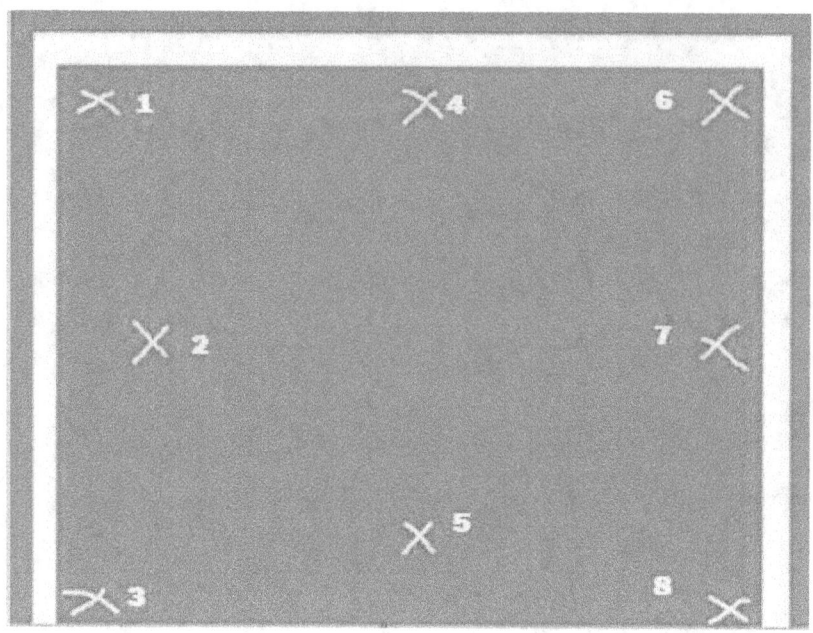

Date:

	Spot 1	Spot 2	Spot 3	Spot 4	Spot 5	Spot 6	Spot 7	Spot 8
Hit area and scored								
Hit area and saved								
Missed area								

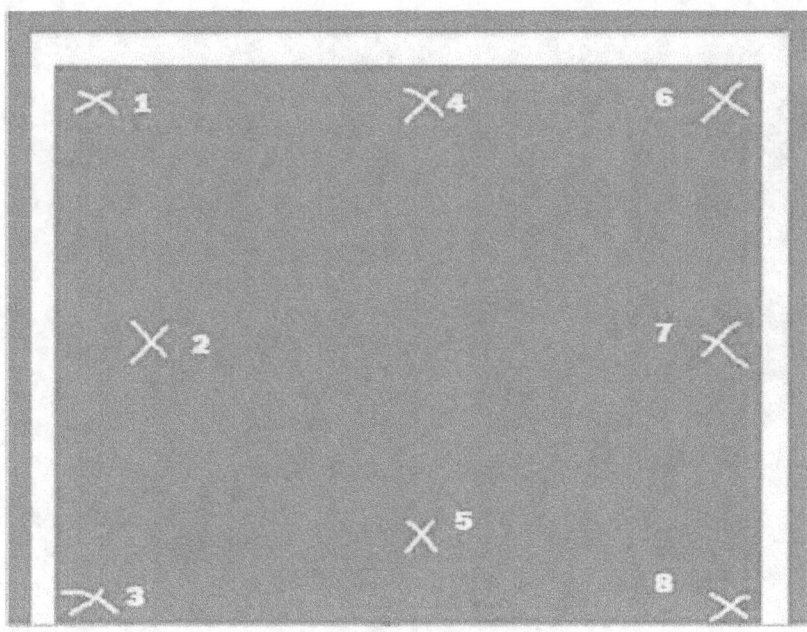

Date:

	Spot 1	Spot 2	Spot 3	Spot 4	Spot 5	Spot 6	Spot 7	Spot 8
Hit area and scored								
Hit area and saved								
Missed area								

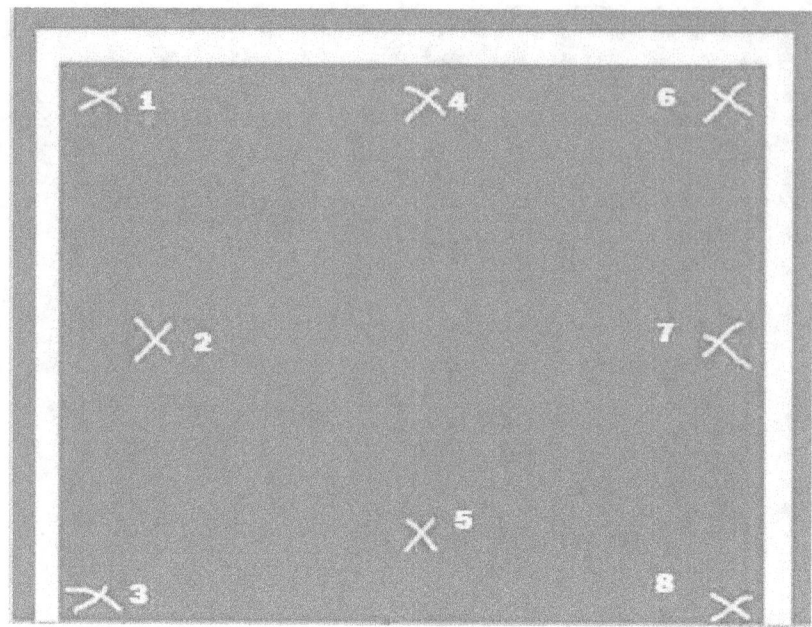

Date:

	Spot 1	Spot 2	Spot 3	Spot 4	Spot 5	Spot 6	Spot 7	Spot 8
Hit area and scored								
Hit area and saved								
Missed area								

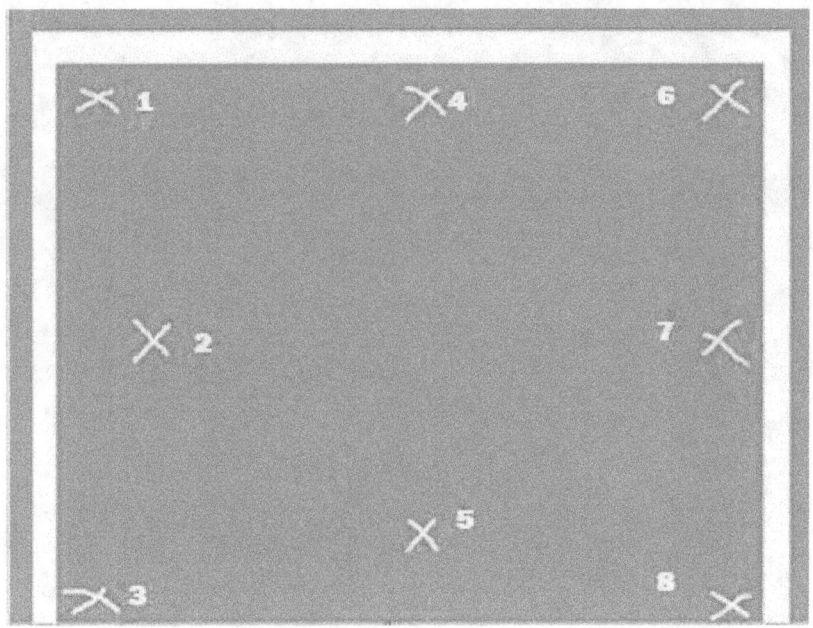

Date:

	Spot 1	Spot 2	Spot 3	Spot 4	Spot 5	Spot 6	Spot 7	Spot 8
Hit area and scored								
Hit area and saved								
Missed area								

www.ingramcontent.com/pod-product-compliance
Lightning Source LLC
Chambersburg PA
CBHW050717090526
44588CB00014B/2322